SIGMUND FREUD AND
HIS CRITIQUE OF RELIGION

SIGMUND FREUD AND HIS CRITIQUE OF RELIGION

Joachim Scharfenberg

Translated by O. C. Dean, Jr.

FORTRESS PRESS   **PHILADELPHIA**

To my wife
with gratitude

Translated from the German *Sigmund Freud und seine Religionskritik als Herausforderung für den christlichen Glauben,* 4th ed. (1976) copyright © 1968 Vandenhoeck & Ruprecht, Göttingen, West Germany.

Library of Congress Cataloging-in-Publication Data

Scharfenberg, Joachim, 1927–
  Sigmund Freud and his critique of religion.
  Translation of: Sigmund Freud und seine Religionskritik als Herausforderung für den christlichen Glauben.
    1. Freud, Sigmund, 1856–1939—Views on religion. I. Title.
  BF173.F85S2813   200'.1'9   87–45002
  ISBN 0-8006-0848-8

2514E87   Printed in the United States of America   1–848

CONTENTS

CONTENTS

TRANSLATOR'S PREFACE

Unless people living in the last part of the twentieth century happen to read a biography or biographical novel (such as Irving Stone's *Passions of the Mind*) or undertake a serious study of Sigmund Freud's writings, they are seldom aware of the revolution that Freud initiated less than a century ago, a revolution in understanding the human mind and in therapeutic approaches to its disorders. Even though others have gone on to expand and, in some cases, to correct his work, it still provides the solid foundation on which current theories and therapies are based. Not only psychology and psychiatry but also theology and, especially, pastoral care have benefited greatly from his discoveries, as Joachim Scharfenberg has attempted to demonstrate in his *Pastoral Care as Dialogue*. It is a thesis of the present volume, however, that theology and the church have yet to treat Freud with the seriousness and thoroughness he deserves and to benefit fully from his theories and perceptions. To this end Scharfenberg seeks to provide a basic understanding of Freud as a person, a scientist, and a therapist, and to deal with his criticism of religion, as well as with theology's criticism of him.

The following work was written as the author's *Habilitationsschrift*, which is a second dissertation required in Germany to qualify as a university lecturer. The thorough research that lies behind the book is evidenced in the original by almost a thousand footnotes and a bibliography of 225 works. For most American readers, however, these primarily German sources would be largely inaccessible, and their inclusion might serve only to discourage the prospective reader. Thus the translator was faced with the problem of how much of the extensive documentation to include. I have sought to resolve the question by presenting primarily the sources that were originally in English, supplemented by English translations of some of the more important German works, the foremost of which is *The Standard Edition* of Freud's work.

Because of the author's desire to let Freud "speak extensively for himself," many passages are veritable tapestries of quotations from Freud. In these cases, as in other quotations from German sources, the translations are mine, since the tracking-down of literally hundreds of references in standard English translations was simply not feasible. For the most part, I have followed the Freudian terminology of *The Standard Edition*, insofar as it could be determined, as well as the standard English titles of Freud's works. Nevertheless, a few general comments on language are in order.

In English one tends to think of the adjectives "spiritual," "mental," and "psychic," as well as the nouns "spirit," "soul," "mind," and "psyche," as designating more or less different things. In German, and especially in Freud, such distinctions are much less clear. For example, *seelisch*, "spiritual" (derived from *Seele*, "soul"), is regularly used by Freud to mean "mental" and is equivalent to *psychisch*, "psychic." And *Seelentätigkeit*, literally, "activities of the soul," is used interchangeably with *Geistestätigkeit*, "activities of the mind or spirit," to mean "mental (= psychic) activity." Therefore, one should keep this semantic similarity in mind and not attach too great a significance to the choice of English terms.

Much of the theological world's hostility toward Freud was rooted in "ideological suspicion," *Weltanschauungsverdacht*. While the German *Weltanschauung*, "world view," is also sometimes used in English, the need for an adjectival form forced me to seek a different English word. The terms "ideology" and "ideological" were chosen because the Merriam-Webster definition of "ideology" as a "systematic body of concepts esp. about human life or culture" (*Webster's New Ninth Collegiate Dictionary*) accords well with the use of *Weltanschauung* in the book and also with Freud's reported understanding of the word as an "intellectual construction that solves all the problems of our existence uniformly under one super-ordinated assumption" (p. 36 below).

In *The Standard Edition* the term *Energiebesetzung* is translated as "cathexis," a term that the general editor, James Strachey, coined from the Greek equivalent of *besetzen*, "to occupy or possess" (and one which, incidentally, did not please Freud). Put off by the foreign coinage and inspired by Merriam-Webster's definition of "cathexis," I have rendered the German term as "investment of emotional energy."

The use of masculine gender forms as common gender, referring to both male and female, is still quite acceptable in the German of today, as it was in Freud's time. While I have not felt that it would be wise or faithful to the original to force inclusive language onto the text, I have avoided the generic use of "man" and "mankind" and tried to keep to a minimum the number of masculine generic pronouns.

Finally, in regard to both the present work and the companion translation of the author's *Pastoral Care as Dialogue*, I would like to express my gratitude to Professor Ludwig Uhlig of the University of Georgia for help with troublesome points in the German, and to my wife, Manita, for proofreading and for help with troublesome points in my English.

O. C. DEAN, JR.

PREFACE TO THE
SECOND EDITION

That this book has required a second edition in so short a time shows that it apparently has been able to meet a need for information. I have left the text essentially unaltered, since the reviews have scarcely conveyed new viewpoints and suggestions. Since a Scandinavian theologian wrote that he felt the book to be a kind of appetizer, I can only offer the hope that in the not too distant future I will be able to serve the main course. I think, however, that others will already be involved. Other theological critics have thought that I overestimated the similarity of Freud's introduction of language as a means of therapy to the "linguistic event" of Ernst Fuchs. That has become more and more clear to me also, without my seeing it, however, as a sufficient reason for revising the text. Only at one point have I undertaken modifications: psychotherapists who feel indebted to the lifework of C. G. Jung have very emphatically called my attention to the fact that passages in which I attempted to present Freud's differences with Jung could be misunderstood as a venture on my part to initiate a polemic against Jung. This, however, was in no way a part of the original intention of this book—not because I felt that there was nothing in Jung against which to polemize (!) but only because I felt it should happen in a form appropriate to the magnitude of the concern. In connection with the present book, in any case, it serves no purpose. I have therefore tried to guard the relevant sections somewhat more strongly against such a misunderstanding.

PREFACE TO THE SECOND EDITION

At this point I would also like to thank my students at Tübingen, who through their critical questions have obliged me to consider further and articulate more clearly the theological consequences of this initial effort. I sincerely hope that the work can be taken further at this point.

Tübingen/Oferdingen   JOACHIM SCHARFENBERG
November 1969

PREFACE TO THE
FIRST EDITION

Not long ago the American theologian Harvey Cox indicated that
theology today has been left in the position of trying to stand with
one foot in the contradictory history of Israel—old and new—and
the other in the lively context of the free, secular individual in the
second half of the twentieth century. Among the dialogue partners
of theology in the "new Israel," Karl Marx and Ernst Bloch are
names on many tongues; by contrast, only here and there does one
hear a third name: Sigmund Freud. In the realm of theology he is
something of a new discovery, yet many feel that they have long
since finished with him.

The following work attempts to see Freud through the eyes of a
theologian and, indeed, one whose acquaintance with psychoanalysis is not a purely literary one but who has himself undergone
psychoanalytical training and has tested the effectiveness of
Freudian theories in psychoanalytical practice. At the same time I
have endeavored to understand Freud on the basis of his own presuppositions. The extent to which I have succeeded will be shown
by authoritative criticism, from which I would gladly learn. The
theological consequences that result from dealing with Freud are, it
seems to me, considerable. Although they could not be spelled out
in this book, an idea of their direction could at least be indicated for
the experts. The examples of Rudolf Bultmann and Ernst Fuchs
were selected because psychoanalysis has scarcely been viewed
from the hermeneutical standpoint, and I would like very much to

show that Freud can certainly accomplish as much for theology as Heidegger has done. May the resulting suggestions and possibilities be taken up in manifold ways by others! My initial concerns are to set right the theological picture of Freud and to prepare material that, with the aid of scientific means, can easily be developed even further.

I must thank those who introduced me to the conceptual world of Freud and through many discussions deepened my knowledge. I name, first of all, the late Carl Müller-Braunschweig and Gustav Bally; then, Robert N. Leslie, of Berkeley; Marie-Louise Werner, of Berlin; Gerhard Scheunert, of Hamburg; and Wolfgang Loch, of Tübingen.

As *Habilitationsschrift* for the attainment of the *venia legendi* for the discipline of "practical theology," this work was accepted by the Protestant Theological Faculty of the University of Tübingen. For this I am grateful to them, as well as to Professor Dietrich Rössler and Professor Werner Jetter for a great deal of criticism and encouragement.

I am also grateful to my tireless co-worker Barbara Schneider, as well as to Hermann Böckenförde, for help with the preparation of the manuscript and with the corrections.

Tübingen/Oferdingen   JOACHIM SCHARFENBERG
September 1968

xiv

INTRODUCTION

When Ludwig Feuerbach hurled his criticism of religion against the world of theologians more than a hundred years ago, only a few thought that his arguments had to be taken seriously. Nevertheless, he was accorded the honor of detailed and comprehensive theological refutation. A quarter century later one could, with Karl Barth, read and interpret him as basically having done theology a great favor by pointing out the dubious nature of many religious manifestations.

Among those who, in their criticism of religion, have followed Feuerbach, Sigmund Freud stands out above all the rest in regard both to intellectual greatness and to popularity and influence. He has still not been accorded the honor of a theological refutation, yet even some theologians are now beginning to approach the question of whether his conceptual model does not have something important to offer to theology, and especially to the discipline of practical theology.

To be sure, some ponderous difficulties stand in the way of opening the topic of Freud to theological discussion. For decades he was despised and ostracized in Germany, and his work still seems to lie buried under mountains of prejudice. In addition, the greater part of Freud's writings—apart from his later works—were produced in a form that was designed for a readership of doctors and psychologists, with the intention of providing help in the treatment of the sick. It is no wonder, then, if the theologian rejects getting to

1

know this material, with the understandable argument that the line must, indeed, be drawn somewhere between theology and its neighboring disciplines if theology is not to lose sight of its real purpose.

Theology—especially practical theology—must, however, always perceive itself to some extent as being the advocate of the world vis-à-vis the church; that is, it must ask itself ever-anew what changes are taking place in the world and what intellectual forces condition and cause those changes. Now, no one can question the fact that conceptual impulses that go back to the psychoanalysis of Freud have today been popularized in both comprehensible and incomprehensible ways and have penetrated into the basic structure of such important disciplines as sociology—indeed, that in general they can be said to determine contemporary feelings about life more strongly than other philosophical trends, including existentialism.

The antipsychological affect, which since the time of the unhealthy psychologizing of faith has dominated theological thinking, seems gradually to be losing its intensity. If Rudolf Bultmann has impressively shown that theology cannot get along without philosophy, then the same is certainly also true for psychology. Here too we will have to decide whether in the future we want to get by in this area with makeshift devices, or whether we are better advised to incorporate the findings of the leading psychological experts into theological discussion and come to terms with them. The more we find in them those conceptual structures around which theology itself is formed—namely, those of the Bible—the easier they will be to rely on.

The following work attempts to demonstrate that this is, to a certain degree, more strongly the case with Freud than with Jung, who is bound to a more "Greek-like" conceptual structure. This book is intended as a modest work preliminary to a future, but absolutely necessary, theological dialogue with Freud. Therefore, it lets him speak extensively for himself. Perhaps it succeeds at least in helping to demolish some of the persisting prejudices.

1

PRELIMINARY QUESTIONS

Freud in the Mirror of Theological Literature

OSKAR PFISTER

For the journey of Sigmund Freud's psychoanalysis into the theological camp and for the picture of him that is reflected in the theological literature, it may have been of fateful significance that the Zurich pastor Oskar Pfister (1873–1956) happened upon Freud's *Traumdeutung* (The interpretation of dreams) in the year 1908. A few years earlier Pfister had expressed his disappointment over the fact that the science of theology was apparently not in a position to make redemption, rebirth, and sanctification understandable to the modern person, and he had turned down a call to a professorial chair in practical theology. With one stroke, the reading of Freud's writing opened up for him a horizon of understanding that he had so painfully missed in his previous pedagogical and pastoral practice. He came to see that behind the incomprehensible actions of young people—such as lying, stealing, compulsive shameful thoughts, depression, and even the inclination toward suicide—lay unconscious motives that could be opened up and understood through an intensive delving into the childhood history of the person concerned. At the same time, however, such a deepened understanding contained the key to relieving these symptoms, which he had earlier considered "moral defects." He was now able successfully to eliminate them in his pedagogical practice and also to publish his results. Out of gratitude he sent to Freud, to whom he owed this success, a special printing of his publication, which included recognition of his debt, and thus was laid the cornerstone of a friendship that was to last thirty years.

What had succeeded for Pfister in pedagogy he now applied in his pastoral practice. Here it was a question, in the first instance, of a young man who had been brought to the verge of suicide by an enthusiastic infatuation from afar and who, out of guilt feelings because of his "uncleanness," wanted to convert to Roman Catholicism. By uncovering and working through unconscious problems relating to the young man's mother, Pfister succeeded in leading this case to a satisfactory resolution.

Pfister took what had proved itself in the practice of pastoral care and, as a theologian working in scholarly fashion, immediately applied it also to incomprehensible elements in church history, even in the text of the New Testament. Thus he was able to show conclusively, for example, how the highly scurrilous and strange piety of Count Zinzendorf suddenly became understandable in the light of the theory of sexual repression. Even the puzzling phenomenon of religious glossolalia, which had been brought into Pfister's pastoral care, could be elucidated with the help of Freud's theory of the unconscious.

Thus it is no wonder that Pfister at first saw and judged Freud's teachings exclusively from a methodological viewpoint; yet, hidden in them, he believed, was a psychology of religion that with "great certainty and thoroughness could sort out even the most tangled threads of faith formation and explain aberrations of faith that had previously been regarded with astonishment and the most helpless lack of understanding." Also exclusively from this predominant viewpoint was Pfister's first great discussion of the whole complex of psychoanalysis (in *Die psychoanalytische Methode* [1913; ET: *The Psychoanalytic Method*]), which he described as a "method that is becoming, struggling for knowledge, and steadily expanding its sphere of influence through a large expenditure of energy."

In this important and often reprinted work, which was highly praised by Freud, Pfister undertook something like an epistemological organization of psychoanalysis,[1] because he considered it primarily from the standpoint of comprehension. The idea of a theological discussion with Freud, however, did not occur to him at all, for it was not at all the task of psychoanalysis as method to provide elucidation of the truth content of religion, to say nothing of passing judgment on it. In any case, it could be granted that psychoanalysis knew better how to understand pathological religious manifestations and how to do away with those forms of religion that must be termed neurotic because they cannot stand up to what Pfister, following Freud's "reality principle," called "reality thinking."

At first, it did not occur to Pfister that this critical function of psychoanalysis in regard to religion, which took the reality principle as its standard, could be used against the biblical sources themselves. He turned instead to a typical phenomenon of the time, the sensation-stirring turmoil that the Indian sadhu Sundar Singh created wherever he went, causing a considerable rustling of leaves in the Christian forest. The work that Pfister accomplished with the related documents must be designated a museum piece of historical-critical research. He had already declared his allegiance to this kind of work before he became acquainted with psychoanalysis,[2] and he saw its comprehending and clarifying treatment of material realized in psychology, in the writing of history, and exemplarily in biblical criticism. Beyond that, what psychoanalysis can achieve is real understanding that does not promote superstition, which can only be harmful to sound faith. Thus it serves a truly evangelical knowledge of salvation, which clearly separates fantasy from reality and therefore can only reject any kind of mania for miracles. For this purpose Pfister applied to the available documents all the means of historical-critical textual research and proved convincingly, conclusively, and point for point, what was to be stricken as legend from the miraculous character of the reports circulating about the "sadhu." Still he did not want to stop with this reductive outcome; for him more was at stake: "Now we must move in the opposite direction and ask, How did those great exaggerations of insignificant events and those fabrications of miracle stories come about?" With the help of psychoanalysis he sought out these conditions of origination. In the case of Sundar Singh, they produced for him the catchwords "derealization of reality," "losses of memory," and "hyperrealization,"[3] by which he meant an unconscious investing of fantasies with the character of reality. Yet for Pfister the astonishing result of such "critical disintegration" was that, even so, he frankly believed in those "who could be deeply edified by Sundar's religious talk in spite of all objections."[4]

If the highly talented Pfister had devoted himself to the textual criticism and hermeneutics of biblical sources with the scholarly tools that he demonstrated in his book on Sundar, he would perhaps have become one of the great figures among researchers into the conditions for understanding the New Testament. His name would be mentioned in the same breath with, say, that of Rudolf Bultmann, to whom he felt close theologically, and that of Albert Schweitzer, who was a personal friend, and the incorporation of psychoanalysis into the realm of theology would have proceeded along different paths and under substantially more favorable auspices. Yet Pfister felt himself pushed in another direction, which may have been influenced in no small degree by the increasingly powerful resounding chorus of theological opposition against psychoanalysis, and which caused him repeatedly to turn down calls to academic office. Instead of that, he thought of himself as, and lived more and more in the role of, an apologist for psychoanalysis vis-à-vis its gang of theological opponents, who were not exactly sparing with malice and slander, and he let them prescribe his course of action. Because Freud's personal lack of religion was repeatedly the target of such attacks, Pfister saw himself compelled to demonstrate the compatibility of psychoanalysis with the "highest ethical and religious demands." He attempted this by pointing out that Freud's own personal renunciation of religion had, indeed, occurred long before the development of psychoanalysis and could not be blamed on it. Above all, however, he concentrated on the central idea of Freudian thinking, the concept of libido, which he sought to expand in the sense of the New Testament commandment to love and the Augustinian concept of love (*caritas*). To his delight, Freud followed this suggestion and in his later work steadily broadened his original understanding of sexuality, which was narrowly biological.

As early as the middle of World War I—which Pfister experienced as a frightening upheaval of destruction and aggressiveness—he received, as if through inspiration, the following commission: "You are to do your little bit through the scientific investigation of love in all its dimensions." In ever new approaches he examined the question of why, again and again, the realization of love in the various developmental stages of the individual and of society was so appallingly unsuccessful.[5] He was so filled with this task that he renounced any further involvement in theological discussion, and when he finally, in a monumental work, investigated the inhibition of love in the Bible and in church history—which he believed he had to write as a "pathological history of Christianity"—the work stood there completely unrelated to contemporary theological activity. Because of his methodological inadequacy, which was not consistent with his earlier scholarship, this work was intentionally ignored by professional theologians.

For theologians who worked in a scholarly fashion, however, the primary reason that it must have seemed awkward to become more closely involved with Pfister and the "psychoanalytic pastoral care" he represented was his naive Jesus-piety, in the dress of which he attempted to make his efforts more palatable to the theologians. He constructed something like a "genuinely Christian religion," into which he incorporated psychoanalysis as a "natural hygiene." It was supposed to loose bonds, clear away debris, and could be designated quite naively and unguardedly the "analytical practice of redemption."[6] From the highly one-sided viewpoint of libido development, the Christian faith was seen almost exclusively in its function of spiritual hygiene; and Christianity's claim to absoluteness was supported with the amazing argument that it is the only religion that guides the libido into the three "proper" channels: love of God, love of neighbor, and love of self. The perfection of this argument is demonstrated, unfortunately, by extolling the love of God as the "flight into the kingdom of ideals," as a "refuge for the longing that is not stilled by the surrounding reality."[7] Thus Pfister made the adventurous attempt to find the basic outline of psychoanalysis already sketched out in Jesus. In him Pfister found the piety of the most healthy and profound of people, whereas Paul and the Johannine texts appeared to him to exhibit a neurotic's kind of piety. The endeavor to put Jesus and Freud on the same plane must have struck academic theologians as an absurdity; to the pious, however, it must have seemed blasphemy.[8]

Pfister maintained this line even into old age, and it pained him deeply that he found so little understanding on the part of theologians. Above all, it grieved him that his much-admired Eduard Thurneysen dismissed him so quickly, called his lifework theologically questionable, and regarded its Christian substance as shriveled to a few rudiments of ethics. In his last longer work, a piece on Calvin, Pfister looked without comprehension at the reformer's theology and programmatically set against it his naive picture of Jesus.

Yet even more unsalutary, no doubt, in its effects on the theological dialogue with psychoanalysis was the fact that Pfister himself felt forced into a polemical disagreement with Freud. It was conjured up by the specter of a suspicion in regard to ideology that had emerged with increasing frequency in the polemic against psychoanalysis and, in view of some publications from the inner circle of psychoanalysts, had to be considered justified. Pfister expressed to Freud his concern in this matter; the idea that psychoanalysis should lead to a new ideology (*Weltanschauung*) was something Pfister could not and would not grant in any event. Freud answered with his work *Die Zukunft einer Illusion* (The future of an illusion), probably the harshest polemic against every form of religion to have appeared since Ludwig Feuerbach. It appeared with an expression of regret that it would grieve his dear friend. Pfister confronted Freud with quick wit and energy. In his reply, "Die Illusion einer Zukunft" (The illusion of a future), Pfister pointed out to Freud his "negative dogmatism," which, "on the evidence of unconscious roots, infers the illusionary character of religion." From then on he never grew tired of rejecting Freud's ideology but, even so, praised psychoanalysis still more highly as method. This discussion seemed possible to Pfister because he interpreted Freud's open antipathy to metaphysics to mean that the latter was devoid of philosophical understanding, and therefore to him any dialogue on this level seemed meaningless.[9] In this, however, Pfister completely failed to recognize that with Freud's turning to "metapsychological speculations"—and that means at the latest with his 1920 work "Jenseits des Lustprinzips" (Beyond the pleasure principle)—he had left the area of empirical psychological research and had gone over to a profound philosophical interpretation of his own findings. Therefore Pfister did not take into account at all Freud's late metapsychological work. He followed it neither in the central teaching of the authorities of id, ego, and superego nor in the theory of the death instinct.

The friendship between the two, nonetheless, remained unbroken until Freud's death, and in Pfister's strange pastoral care, which Freud accepted with a sense of humor, Freud got to hear many kinds of pleasant and unpleasant things: that he had fallen victim to the dangerous illusion of the ideology of those without an ideology, that he had created an ersatz religion in the form of "Enlightenment thinking of the eighteenth century in a proud modern renovation," but also that he had actually lived something like an unconscious Christianity.[10] Pfister held up to him—certainly not without justification—the word of Nietzsche that it is indeed upon a metaphysical faith that faith in science still rests, and that even the godless and those opposed to metaphysics take from the fire which a thousand-year-old faith ignited. Yet he emphasized repeatedly that from the first to the last encounter, he had stood diametrically opposed to Freud in regard to ideology.[11] Thus anyone who made Freud's acquaintance primarily through Pfister— and that seems to have been a whole generation of theologians and pastors—knows only the "early Freud," a Freud whose later work is completely suppressed. Hence Freud was pushed aside into the realm of therapeutic methodology, and for decades the philosophical and even theological relevance of his ways of thinking remained undiscovered.

THE "RESISTANCE"

An overview of the polemical disagreement that Freud experienced from the theological side during his lifetime might evoke a question from the unprejudiced and psychoanalytically uninformed reader: Why was this polemic played out on such a shockingly low plane, remaining largely in the realm of the emotional, and hardly any attempt made to press forward to an objective dialogue? One must realize, however, that this was exactly Freud's intention. In contrast to Pfister, he in no way attempted to recommend psychoanalysis persuasively and to make it pleasing to a broad public. Moreover, he saw his publications much too much from the standpoint of a therapeutic process in relation to society. Just as, in the individual therapeutic process, he most decisively rejected any effect by suggestion and strove for a lasting cure by first provoking resistance, exposing it in sharp outline, making it conscious, and working through it, Freud likewise believed that, in the work of psychoanalysis with the public, the resistance of the reader must first be provoked and mobilized if a real clarification is to come about. Vis-à-vis the physicians and theologians, however, he followed yet another intention: he did all he could to keep them away from psychoanalysis. He hoped, that in the future, psychoanalysis would have its own professional status, which it did not in his time, that of a kind of "secular pastor who does not need to be a doctor and is not allowed to be a priest." He wrote two of his works, *Die Frage der Laienanalyse* (The question of lay analysis; 1926) and *Die Zukunft einer Illusion* (1927), for the sole, decided purpose of frightening away these two groups: "In the first, I want to protect analysis from the physicians; in the second, from the priests." One cannot argue with the fact that this intention of Freud's was extremely successful. Over the decades bitter resistance against psychoanalysis came, especially in Germany, from the medical and theological camps. For that very reason it will not be superfluous to take a close look at these two forms of resistance in their conscious and unconscious motivation.

Whoever expects a richly differentiated, penetrating, and objective polemic will, of course, be disappointed. There are only a few reproaches and themes, which recur with tiring monotony and which, in complete contrast to usual scholarly custom, one writer seems to take over from another. They rely on a few authorities, to whom the provenience of individual arguments can be easily traced. In addition to Pfister, these include, above all, the Berlin pastor Ernst Jahn, who has spoken up repeatedly from the beginnings of psychoanalysis until the present day. He happened very early into the circle of Alfred Adler's friends and followers and, through the animosity between Freud and Adler, apparently blocked his own access to an objective knowledge of psychoanalysis. To prove even more effective was the book of Paul Maag, a Christian doctor and psychotherapist; the theologians were apparently confident that as an expert he was reliably informed.[12] His book gives the appearance of objectivity, since it lets Freud speak for himself and also repeatedly purports to make all kinds of laudatory statements about him.

Yet at the decisive points it remains uncomprehending and, full of ideological and moralistic prejudices, gives an "accounting" of Freud that sinks to such a shocking level of scholarship that any further discussion of it would be pointless.

Supported by these authorities, two themes, heavily charged with emotion, are expounded again and again: First, there is a trembling apprehension about all higher things in humanity, which clearly includes an anxiety about a correction of one's own self-understanding. Second, there is a resistance to the ongoing secularization process, particularly in pastoral care, because it makes ecclesiastical practice seem questionable and could shake up tenaciously defended positions within a "pitiful rearguard action" (Freud).

Such was the case especially where one still moved along the paths of the "old" theology and where the confession of Franz Delitzsch remained unforgotten: "that spirit and body in principle are of different origin and essence," and that this is a doctrine "by which we live and die." In these ranks Freud's psychologism must have been looked upon as if he were abetting a widespread contemporary illness, namely, the "relativization of all norms and values." Against all appearances, it was asserted that psychoanalysis brings absolutely no real help and assurance; this can be done only by pastoral care, which really banishes fear and anxiety and thereby shows its superiority. Through psychoanalysis, indeed, the poor sick person is only maneuvered out of self-centeredness to doctor-centeredness, but what he needs is, rather, encouragement, strengthened will, confidence, and these are to be drawn from the spirit-filled realm of pastoral care.[13] Most decisively rejected were the "arbitrary acts" and "fantasies" of psychoanalysis; critics diagnosed "gross aberrations" and saw the danger of a "soul-poisoning" effect infinitely increased, because the highest ethical values were endangered. When systematic treatments of pastoral care were finally composed, their authors argued long and hard with Freud but did not even make the effort to recapitulate correctly to any extent the basic concepts of psychoanalysis—to say nothing of these writers' grotesque assertions and imputations.[14] They inveighed strenuously against the dangers of making conscious the things that tear down breeding and custom, they saw as the task of pastoral care

11

the creation of inhibitions, and they appealed for the most shameless exploitation of guilt feelings resulting from "self-abuse." One can easily understand that when these pastoral-care texts appeared, the only reaction from Freud and his followers to this kind of polemic was icy silence. Otto Haendler certainly had every reason to warn the pastor against a "maliciously disparaging attitude" in regard to Freud.[15]

Yet even in the camp of dialectical and neo-Reformation theology, the figure of Freud aroused considerable negative feeling. Karl Barth saw theology already sinking "in the gruesome morass of the psychology of the unconscious." He rejected fundamentally the idea of his receiving from depth psychology information of any kind about anthropological situations and relationships. Although he maintained that Freud must be placed on the same level as Nietzsche and Heidegger, he regretted that with Freud, human nature "comes down to the common denominator of the very specifically sexual." From the standpoint of intellectual history, however, Barth thought that the files on the case of Freud had already been closed for thirty or forty years. For the rest, he held to his rule, highly worth taking to heart, that in matters of psychotherapy, only those who understood something of the subject should enter the discussion. Emil Brunner, in the zeal of his settling accounts with any form of psychology, did not notice that psychoanalysis, compared with the traditional psychology of religion, represented something very new and different. He protested in the name of the Spirit against its empirical-causal methods that take as actually given what can only be understood as entelechy; it must be maintained, however, that what faith is all about is "indeed precisely the radical ignorance in principle of all inner processes." Behind Freud's libido theory Brunner presumed an ersatz religion, for through the justification of the individual as a sexual being, Freud had created the main idea for the practice of a sexual religion. Therefore, here also the consequences for pastoral care can consist only in questioning the healing successes of psychoanalysis ("Why, then, does one not heal with living piety through faith in Christ?"). For the believer, its application can only be felt as an outrage against one's soul.

A different tone was set by theology more strongly defined by Lutheranism. It asserted above all that psychoanalysis strives for a kind of self-forgiveness that seeks through all means to achieve for a person a calmness of the soul, and it believed that "the satanic is near!"[16] Only because of an ill feeling of competition, which was extremely widespread on the part of theologians and pastors, is it understandable that psychoanalysis was calculated with malicious gloating to have made just as many blunders as the church's pastoral care; and it took a great deal of impertinence and naiveté to present psychoanalysis to the theological public as only raking up muck with its interrogatory method and merely cultivating autism through quick forgiveness. The right to operate was granted only to the psychotherapist "who worked with a complete understanding of religious experiences and sacramental values, if not in joyful affirmation of the church." Only a "filling up" with Christian religious values could give psychoanalysis any chance for effectiveness, for the Bible—it was rashly asserted—offers a still deeper depth psychology than the "spiritual anesthesia" of psychoanalysis, with its innocuous language, and Paul had practiced an even more fearful psychoanalysis than Freud.

The fairest and most painstaking attempt to understand Freud and do justice to him came from the ranks of Scandinavian Lutheran theology. Arvid Runestam at least saw and gave recognition to the fact that psychoanalysis placed its efforts under the heading of "freedom from the law" and thus had taken up "an early evangelical concern." Also the demand for relativity and accommodation of the moral demand was greeted as a legitimate Christian claim. But to turn oneself over to love as the frame of reference for the ethical demand, according to Runestam, went too far, for life's floods of love could also lead to immorality, and the absolute nature of the commandment could be surrendered. And thus the moralistic argument also dominated here: there was a fear that psychoanalysis granted a dispensation from guilt that meant a threat to the religious and moral future, and the fact that Freud regarded "transference" as a normal component of psychoanalytic treatment was characteristically used for the moral defamation of psychoanalysts, with the pastor naturally rejecting such an "infatuation." One could make sense of the psychoanalytic theory of repression only if—contrary to clinical experience—one could decide on a reversal of its results and begin to speak of the repression of moral and religious forces as the cause of neurosis.

13

Finally, in the teachings on pastoral care defined more by the new pietism, one is ready, if need be, to grant to psychoanalysis a kind of tactical significance. It is only for people who do not want to get into anything at all religious. Naturally, it can lead to success only if it crosses over into the religious and metaphysical, for only through the religious realm are changes in life possible.

Thus Freud appears as the great undoer of ethics and morality, who conjures up the horrible danger of secular competition with pastoral care. The resistance of the theologians to psychoanalysis, emotionally defined by this image, would probably determine pastoral care today even more strongly if a formula had not been found in the meantime that made possible with a single stroke an amicable coexistence of pastoral care and psychoanalysis.

PSYCHOANALYSIS AS A "HELPING SCIENCE"

How could one better come to terms with the reality of the victorious advances of psychoanalysis on all fronts, exploit its indisputable successes where possible for one's own cause, and yet avoid going too deeply into the disturbing theological questions that resulted from Freud's interpretations of the world and of humanity? That must have been the main question among theologians after the noise of emotionally conditioned polemic had begun to die down. Thurneysen can claim for himself the honor of having effectively answered this question for decades hence when he assigned to psychoanalysis the role of a "helping science" for pastoral care. This redeeming formula was very productive. It made possible a clear separation of jurisdictions, permitted the theologian to hold fast to the fundamental superiority of pastoral methods, and yet turned the practical discoveries of psychoanalysis into fair game: one could help oneself to what was desirable, yet lay the blame for everything one did not like on Freud's biased world view, and reject it now just as before.

According to Thurneysen, pastoral care, in contrast to psychoanalysis, represents "something completely and fundamentally different." This statement was proclaimed with all the pathos and dignity of dogma, so that anyone who called it into question had to fall under the suspicion of being a poor theologian. Thus an iron curtain descended between two different domains that actually have nothing to do with each other. In the one, it is a question of "illness"; in the other, of "need." Pastoral care comes from God (because it is free); psychotherapy comes from human beings (because it costs money).

With one's feet firmly planted on the ground of this distinctive delineation in principle between the two realms, one could then confidently invite the pastor to reach candidly into the arsenal of psychoanalysis and choose what he can use. Psychoanalytic knowledge and techniques (such as attention to errors and dreams) could now be recommended as therapeutic means for "ailing pastoral care." If one could only succeed in discovering the etiological basis of a mental disturbance, its "simple, sure explanation" could also come to light even in pastoral care. Nonetheless, psychoanalysis has at its disposal something "splendidly dynamic" that the pastor can take over without hesitation, a "practical wisdom" that can become a valuable treasury for Christian pastoral care and perhaps even open the doors that lead to faith and to the kingdom of God.

The concept of psychoanalysis as a helping science recognized its status as a science. It could no longer be regarded simply as the "camouflage of a faith achieved, of course, on the lowest level of primitiveness." Thurneysen had to admit that Freud's conceptions had gained acceptance and contained a truth so irrefutable "that its challengers could find no fault with it." Yet in order to be able to preserve the superiority of theology, Thurneysen fell back on Pfister's distinction between method and ideology and reserved for the theologian the right to regard as ideologically suspect everything about psychoanalysis that did not fit his theological framework. This is true, according to Thurneysen, first of all for the "curious predomination of sexuality" in Freud, but especially in regard to the fact that Freud had admittedly developed no overall view of humanity and consequently had no understanding of the deepest personal core of a human being, which could only be circumscribed with the category of mystery and was beyond the grasp of psychological knowledge.

The "dialogue" between theology and psychoanalysis proceeded as follows: on the one hand, with a certain back-patting openness, the analysts were granted their therapeutic successes and the desirability of learning from them, but on the other hand, everything that seemed suspect in regard to ideology was rejected. Without trying to be comprehensive, I mention a few of the things that over the years have fallen victim to theological dismissal: Freud's theory of the Oedipus complex was labeled "simply nonsensical," the teaching about instincts fell under the verdict of an "undetected deification of the sex drive," and it was thought that both could be reduced to the common denominator of an ideology of "autonomous realism" or of "naturalistic-mechanistic thinking." Because Freud's critique of culture rested on the ideology of "pessimistic agnosticism," it was also condemned. The idea that religion and culture could have something to do with sexual denial and sexual repression was a "naturalistic interpretation" that, with an intensified psychology, simply carried completely too far the ideology of a Marx or a Nietzsche, which, of course, was to be rejected. The attempt to understand personal difficulties largely from the person's history fell under the suspicion of an ideology of thinking in terms of causality. Finally, every claim of psychoanalysis to be more than an "individual form of psychological research technique" was regarded, and rejected, as ideologically conditioned.[17] In the Anglo-American world, the terms used to take aim especially at the pleasure principle and the reality principle are "reductive naturalism and secular humanism" (Outler, *Psychotherapy and the Christian Message*, 43, 73, 199). They leave no room for allowing the spiritual capacities of humanity to come into their own (Murray, *Christian Psychotherapy*, 23).

Now, whether a direct theological discussion with Freud was rejected with the old argument that Freud had removed himself from the God-question "expressly and with anger," or with the new argument that he continually injured the personal responsibility of humanity, the task could, in any case, only be formulated as Adolf Allwohn put it: Freud's basic concepts must first be freed from their ideological background and adapted to the Christian anthropology before they can be applied in pastoral care.[18] For—so reads the final judgment—Freud's spiritual roots lie deep in the nineteenth century, and we in our day must reject his spirituality, or rather, his lack of spirituality.[19]

Apart from the doubtfulness of the thesis that Freud must be regarded as a typical figure of the nineteenth century, critical questions are also raised by the program of liberating Freud from his ideological background. Can such a liberation be successfully carried out? We have seen, in this regard, that no central finding of Freud's psychoanalysis is safe from critical dismissal by the theologians and the whole thing dwindles to nothing. Walter Uhsadel is certainly correct when he calls such a process "methodologically dishonest."[20] Also, this effort, repeatedly undertaken since Pfister's time, must be questioned with respect to its success. In his large history of pastoral care, Charles Kemp stated in regard to American churches, so well known for their progressiveness, that even in 1947 there had still been no serious efforts undertaken on the part of the vast majority of the clergy to study and really understand psychoanalysis and to relate it to the practical work of their ministry (Kemp, *Physicians*, 90). And even in the present, Paul Ricoeur has asserted that in the area of the solace that pastoral care is supposed to bring, "the teachings of psychoanalysis have not been used at all." They have, of course, already strengthened the faith of unbelievers, "yet scarcely begun to clarify the faith of the faithful."

Our chapter that attempts to give an overview of the picture of Freud in the theological literature would have to close with this distressing observation if we could not point to a few theologians in more recent times who are trying to lead the challenge of a discussion with Freud onto more appropriate paths.

THE ACCEPTANCE OF THE CHALLENGE

The fact that Freud could also be called a "good gift of God to the human race," indeed, that someone fascinated by him could see it as a sign of grace that Freud apparently wanted to have psychoanalysis conducted by the pastor rather than by the doctor (Murray, *Christian Psychotherapy*, 13), shows that there is another side to our problem. The modicum of enthusiasm for Freud among theologians, which can doubtless be observed here and there, is still not sufficient for a genuine interaction with psychoanalysis. That point will be reached when a serious effort is made to understand Freud—and, of course, the whole Freud, in the sense of his actual intentions—and when his results are brought into a reciprocal, critical dialogue with theological problems and issues.

This seems to have been the case for the first time on a larger scale with the Anglican theologian R. S. Lee, in his book *Freud and*

Christianity. His theological point of departure consists in the perception that the Christian faith itself is subject to a historical process that includes the task of ever more thoroughly cleansing and freeing the faith itself of non-Christian elements. Now, Lee particularly designates as such non-Christian elements all erroneous conceptions of reality that have appeared in the course of history in connection with astronomy, biology, and evolution. When those who represented the faith held fast to such false concepts of reality, it necessarily led to conflict with the natural sciences, and this has always resulted in theology's having to correct its understanding of reality. Yet, according to Lee, this has never actually led to a loss of Christian substance but has, on the contrary, led to an increase in its correspondence to reality and thus also in its Christian character. Now, it is the task of the present day to take the false anthropological theories that are stubbornly maintained in theology and subject them to a critical examination. In this process the psychoanalysis of Freud is supposed to provide decisive assistance.

Lee sets forth as Freud's most important anthropological perception the observation that a human being apparently has alternative ways of shaping the relationship between the self and reality: according to the world of wishing—in Freud's language, by means of the pleasure principle, which dominates in childhood, in primitive societies, in dreams, and in neurosis—or according to the real world through the reality principle. Where reality does not reign, fantasy reigns. Yet this is what takes away freedom and throws a person into bondage. According to Freud, only freedom from one's own fantasies can help one to the freedom of a conscious ego. Psychoanalysis does this for the individual in the healing process. Lee wants to apply this process to the whole of the Christian faith as a historical manifestation. His decisive question is,

> Is Christianity the expression of a free Ego, dependent on the reality-principle and based on a knowledge of the real world, or is it a product of the unconscious, springing from fantasies and only selecting and using such knowledge as it needs to further its unconscious wishes? (Lee, *Freud and Christianity*, 87)

Just as Freud incorporated the pathway from the pleasure principle to the reality principle into a developmental pattern that leads, in the life of the individual, from childhood to responsible adulthood and, in the life of society on the other hand, from mythical to scientific thinking, so Lee made the maturation process the central concept of his religious critique. Maturation means progression, and that means being able to go free and unburdened from the past into the future. This process can be hindered, for example, when reality offers failures that are too great. Then comes a backward step, a regression to the stage of coping with reality by means of wishful thinking and fantasy. The child believes again in the omnipotence of its thoughts. In the life of society, this corresponds to the magical stage of development.

Here Lee turns the master's method against the master himself by ingeniously proving that even atheism, which Freud purports to advocate, could represent a state of immaturity, that is, the projection of the wish to be rid of the father. In the process, however, the wish slips unconsciously into some other form, and therefore atheism seems to have a certain affinity with authoritarian and totalitarian systems.

Thus psychoanalysis is the very thing that can free the Christian faith and enable it to grow to full strength and maturity:

> If Christianity insists on clinging to neurotic manifestations of the unconscious as true religion for full-grown men and women it dooms itself to be cast aside in man's upward struggle towards the natural goals of freedom, power and love. It will cease to be truly "Christian." (Ibid., 197)

We would like to begin our critique at this point. Lee expressly calls for the criteria that are to be used for the judgment of various religious manifestations to be drawn from psychoanalysis. With this he turns over to psychopathology the decisive question of theology: What then is regarded as Christian or un-Christian? His equations are un-Christian = immature = neurotic; Christian = mature = healthy. Here he will have to prepare himself for the sharpest protest of the theologians. Lee blunts the edge of his otherwise so creditable study by neglecting to demonstrate how Freud, the "completely godless Jew" (as he once called himself), actually appeared suited to make judgments on the Christian or un-Christian character of religious manifestations.

At this point, however, it could be helpful to consider the reflections and comments that another theologian has given in his lifework, incorporating them more aphoristically and occasionally than systematically. Paul Tillich saw very clearly the effective core of resistance against Freud, through which Freud must have had a shocking impact on society. It lay first of all in what many felt to be the threat of psychoanalysis to sexual ethics, then in its antireligious ideas, but above all in the fact that a middle-class, moralistic society cannot endure the uncovering of its unconscious motives. Thus, as we have already tried to show, a large part of the theological polemic against Freud becomes understandable under the psychoanalytic categories of resistance and defense. Tillich also goes into another group of arguments that reject psychoanalysis, which we tried to present under the heading of "ideological suspicion." He demonstrates that the ideas that come from Freud cannot be an ideology, because in their very lack of ideology they have contributed the strongest impulses toward the destruction of the old world view. Tillich rejects the idea of pushing Freud off into the realm of therapy but would rather see him in his appropriate philosophical context.[21] By being put in place in the history of ideas, psychoanalysis loses a lot of the frighteningly singular character ascribed to it; now it can be seen from the standpoint of its characteristic interplay with ontology and sociology, through which—for example in Heidegger and E. Goldstein—the primitive human situation is described as standing under the original powers of anxiety and death. Thus Freud's understanding of humanity moves in line with the existentialist analyses of the human situation that step into the gaps where school philosophy evades the question of historical existence and the determination of thought by fate and, through epistemology and ethics, seeks to convey a feeling of security from fate.

Tillich also gives, however, detailed indications of the theological relevance of Freudian perceptions. Of course, he does not question that these belong in the realm of "usual knowledge," which initially has nothing to do with revealed knowledge. But according to Tillich, this distinction is dissolved in that moment when, so to speak, under the cloak of usual knowledge, things are considered that concern us ultimately. And with Freud, that is constantly the case.

Tillich thought that he could interpret the concept of the unconscious as, in the sense of the later Freud, transcending the purely conceptual and becoming a "symbolic indication of what cannot be named," and thus coming into relationship with the "chaos" of the mythologies and the μὴ ὄν of metaphysical speculations.

For Tillich, Freud's death-wish theory is, as a spiritual phenomenon, the reaction to the meaninglessness of the never-ending and never-satisfied libido. As a most eloquent expression of the existential self-alienation of humanity, it becomes a witness to the ambiguity of life in a profundity that is otherwise reached only by Paul in his word on worldly grief that leads to death (2 Cor. 7:10).

Tillich also gladly took up Freud's description of the "ritual actions" of obsessive-compulsive neurotics, in order to use them to demonstrate the "institutional profanation" of the religious act in the life of the individual. Similarly, the critical function of psychoanalysis toward religion can be made responsible, in the positive sense, for the fact that the churches have largely given up the moralistic perversion of the concept of holiness.

These examples reveal the significance Tillich accorded to Freud in the sphere of Christian faith. For him there can be no more talk of the concern that psychoanalysis will undermine religious symbols. On the contrary, only with its help will they be properly understood. It is thus granted that Freud, in a kind of "alien prophecy," was doing what the church itself is actually supposed to be about. By making the unbiased acceptance of a person the irrevocable presupposition of his therapy, he contributed a great deal toward the reshaping of the intellectual climate in the direction of rediscovering the central gospel of the acceptance of the sinner. Thus Freud can be raised to the rank of a critic of the churches out of the divine Spirit; Tillich held that if the churches do not accept this alien prophecy raised against them, "they will sink into meaninglessness, and the divine spirit will work through ostensibly atheistic and anti-Christian movements."

Hence, we stand before an astonishing reversal of the theological disagreement with Freud. Before, he was the accused and convicted; now, his perceptions can become the critical principle for the attitude of the church, because in them the essence of the gospel is perhaps better lifted up and because they can help achieve a deepened understanding of reality and of the self.[22]

Walter Bernet has also dealt with Freud from this standpoint of understanding reality. He emphatically warns theologians against a purely opportunistic attitude toward the findings of Freud and considers it inappropriate for theologians to burst out with a premature hurrah because medicine has now, all of a sudden, rediscovered the soul. Freud would then be taken seriously only because he expressed ideas that were useful to the Christian theologian. No, Freud's findings should be taken seriously for the sake of their "open objectivity." Not only did they mean a broadening of the sphere of reality that is humanity, by granting the character of reality to the spiritual, but Freud also placed the personal element in the foreground when he emphasized, from his early days on, that in the struggle against resistances within the patient the doctor cannot remain outside the battlefield but rather is drawn in through transference and countertransference. With this, the understanding of illness is raised to the level of the personal, and the wall of objective, scientific thinking within medicine has in principle been breached.

Now, to be sure, Bernet reproached Freud because in his theoretical superstructure he again called into question these findings from his practice. Here again, then, it comes down to an objectifying manipulation of the sphere of reality that is the soul, and thus everything that appears in concrete form retreats behind assumed abstractions. Reality as a whole no longer comes to expression; it becomes objective by losing the temporal aspect of its coming to expression. Language thereby loses its hermeneutical function and becomes purely an instrument for the abstract labeling of things. Thus here again the discussion moves onto the pathways of the old reproach that Freud was enmeshed in the anthropology of the mechanistic natural sciences of his time. With this interpretation of Freud the last word on these issues has probably not been spoken.[23] But what is actually important for our concern has already been revealed: precisely when the linguistic nature of human existence stands at the focus of theological interest, as it does today, the conceptions of Freud become fruitful at the center of theological reflection.

Also of this opinion is Ricoeur, the French philosopher of religion, who attempts to see Freud completely from the hermeneutical standpoint. His spirituality, Ricoeur says, cannot be regarded as at all positivistic; it represents a "reductionist hermeneutics" that pursues the intention of revealing the person to himself as capable of affirmation and creative in meaning. Thus a "colossal event" has become reality: "Through Freud, our culture has accomplished its own self-analysis." His psychoanalysis has to do with the whole human reality and can therefore assume critical functions regarding religion. These must, of course, be gained in a critical interaction with Freud. As their starting point, the parallels that Freud draws between pathological phenomena (obsessive-compulsive neurosis) and religion must be seen not as an assertion about the identity of religion but as an analogy. That gives the religious person the possibility of reflecting on how one can avoid being like one's "distorted doppelgänger," the obsessive-compulsive. Ricoeur sees this possibility in an abandonment of the "compulsion to repeat," in a yes to history and to historicity even in religious existence. Hence it also becomes for him a decisive question whether the direction taken within the faith will be a regressive one that stimulates infantile wishes in endless repetition or a progressive one that can set free a "meaning-discovering power." Psychoanalysis can destroy everything archaic, infantile, and neurotic about guilt feelings in order to set free the authentic meaning of sin; it should distinguish between infantile comfort and "comfort according to the Spirit," which is open only "to the highest degree of obedience in regard to reality." The discussion with Freud should develop a language of faith that no longer corresponds only to wishful thinking as supplication for protection and providence but that suits "interpellation in which I no longer ask anything, but listen."

The preliminary end and high point of this chapter in the history of the theological interpretation of Freud can be seen in Johannes Schreiber, who was the first to dare to designate Freud expressly as a theologian, in order "to take from the wall between theology and psychoanalysis some of its malicious insurmountability." He holds the effort to understand Freud's words in their "actual intention" to be the absolute prerequisite for conveying his meaning for theology. Precisely as a theologian, Schreiber can fully identify with Freud's struggle against the "illusionary conceptual apparatus of religion," because Freud pursued indirectly the goal of understandably bringing to bear the truth contained in religious doctrines. Freud thereby moved into unsuspected closeness to existential interpretation, and Schreiber can even ask the question, whether Freud, "in contrast to many theological currents of his time, did not make radical use of the Reformation's *sola scriptura* without wanting to or being aware of it." By elaborating human love, and not reason, as the highest authority and mainspring of Freud's actions, Schreiber is able to point to the "deepest secret" in Freud's life: his carefully concealed relationship to the Moses figure, in which something like "Freud's poverty of faith" is hidden; and his Godforsakenness, in which he lost every conception of God, yet which gave him the strength for a life of faith, love, and hope, in which he "as a lay theologian anticipated the nonreligious interpretation of the gospel urged by Dietrich Bonhoeffer."

Yet we must ask whether Freud's reception of an "unconscious Christianity" is not advanced here a little too smoothly. Is it not one of the essential attributes of a theologian that he works carefully with his sources? With Freud, however, this care is missing precisely in regard to the sources of the Christian faith. Vis-à-vis Freud, therefore, there can be no uncritical idealization or adoption by theologians but only a critical interaction.

At this point, however, we must break off. What are the conclusions that are to be drawn from our overview of the history of the theological interpretation of Freud? Theology's picture of Freud exhibits astonishing contrasts, tensions, and discrepancies. It shows with humiliating clarity the historically conditioned nature of theological knowledge, into whose relentless progression we must humbly place ourselves with the modicum of knowledge that we are able to derive from our work. Perhaps the following guidelines can be established for a theological discussion of Freud:

1. The separation of psychoanalytic method—which was to be classified as a "helping science" of practical theology—from its ideological background has proved unfruitful. The only possible approach is an interaction with Freud as a whole in his own original intentions.

2. This "Freud as a whole" is comprehensible only as a historical phenomenon. Freud's conceptual world was subjected to a constant

process of change and clarification, and it can be meaningfully described only in the form of lines of development. In this, one must examine whether Freud was actually a typical child of the nineteenth century, where his spiritual roots could lie, and through which interactions he found his own conceptual models. The fruitfulness of these conceptual models should be examined with regard to several theological questions.

3. Freud's most original and unquestionably most characteristic feat was the introduction of language as a means of therapy. What were the consequences for him that resulted from this simple fact?

4. In "bold encroachment" Freud took the knowledge he had gained from individual therapy and applied it to society and culture. For almost all his life he wrestled with the problem of religion and developed ever new conceptions of it, which were not free of errors and misunderstandings.

5. In spite of this, the Freudian critique of religion should be taken seriously. It could prove its fruitfulness in three areas:

(a) The persistent protest that was raised against Freud in the name of traditional morality cannot be traced back only to a simple misunderstanding; it must have real reasons.

(b) Freud's discussion of mythos should be consulted regarding its relevance for the present theological debate.

(c) Freud's classification of human existence as historical existence under the laws of regression and progression could be of special interest for theological reflection that is oriented toward the historical outlook of the Bible.

From these viewpoints come the outline and methodology of the following comments.

2

THE MAN

Freud and His Intellectual Roots

The figure, work, and personality of Freud have left behind an extremely divided impression not only in the literature of theology. Secular biographers have also painted a rather variegated picture. A broad spectrum extends from uncritical hero worship, in the style and pathos of proclamations from veterans organizations, to loathsome attempts, full of malicious gloating and pseudopsychoanalytical captiousness, to drag the most intimate details about this man into the light of day.[1] As a young man Freud must already have had an inkling of something like this, for it was probably more than a lark when, at the age of twenty-eight, he destroyed all his personal papers and drawings for the express purpose of thoroughly confusing his future biographers: "I rejoice already to think of how they will go astray." In any case, concerning intimate details, which he pressed others to reveal, he always remained closemouthed in regard to himself, and Ludwig Marcuse is surely right when he asserts that the most autobiographical traits are to be discovered behind Freud's teachings on resistance. He tried early on to push others (especially Alfred Adler and Jung) to the forefront, to withdraw himself completely behind the work, "our thing," and gradually "to shrink into an ornament."

Yet it is not just Freud's shyness in revealing himself that makes it hard to draw a picture of the creator of psychoanalysis; it is extraordinarily difficult to find a common denominator for his nature and his utterances. Apart from the fact that over the years he subjected his theories to many modifications and could flatly turn them upside down, he almost always had, by his own admission, at least two opinions on everything, and in many areas never resolved this tension; indeed, to him it often appeared to be the very sign of life. Therefore, if there is a leitmotif for Freud's personality as well as for his work, the most likely one is the concept of "ambivalence," coined by Eugen Bleuler and most loved by Freud himself. Only from this point of view can one draw a picture that is to some degree accurate, of Freud's educational background, of his scientific intentions, and of what, in all probability, shaped him in the deepest and most enduring way. I believe such preliminary reflections are indispensable in order to reach a more accurate judgment of Freud's achievement than has evidently been possible for many theologians who have dealt with him previously.

FREUD AS READER AND LEARNER

It strikes one as strange that the religious element clearly predominates in the earliest childhood memories of a man who later wanted to think of himself as a "grave enemy of religion." There was the nursemaid, that old, ugly, but smart woman who told him a lot about God and hell and took him to all the churches, so that when he came home, he preached and told "what God does." There was also, above all, his earliest reading, about which he later said, "As I recognized much later, early preoccupation with the biblical stories, when I had scarcely learned the art of reading, defined in an enduring fashion the direction of my interest."[2] His father later wrote to him that it was in Freud's seventh year "that the spirit of the Almighty overcame you and urged you to learn," and he gave him on his thirty-fifth birthday the Bible in which Freud had earlier read, accompanying it with the urgent admonition

> The spirit of the Almighty is speaking to you and saying, "Read in my book; if you do that, to you will be revealed the sources of knowledge and understanding." . . . In this book you cast your first look at the image of the Almighty. You listened willingly to his teachings and did your best to let yourself be lifted up on the wings of his spirit.

When we hear, by contrast with this, that Freud later asserted repeatedly that he was raised completely without religion, we have one of those ambivalences that are so abundant in Freud's life and work. Indeed, one would even have to wonder whether we cannot observe here that mechanism that Freud so masterly described and named "repression," and whether it is not the power of the "return of the repressed" that allows observance of at least one aspect of his life, namely, that even to his death he never freed himself from the religious phenomenon—more precisely, from the "Moses" phenomenon.[3]

In the first place—and to be sure very early—there are most definitely other influences to be noted besides the religious. At eight years of age Freud read Shakespeare, soon afterward E. Thiers's *Konsulat und Kaiserreich,* which caused him to experience a pronounced militaristic phase, and at thirteen his first modern novels; he remarked that he then had the German classical writers already "behind him." Especially formative for him was his encounter with Cervantes' *Don Quixote,* on which even later he repeatedly "feasted." With his friend Silberstein, and behind the backs of his parents, he learned Spanish; and the two friends developed their own mythology and vocabulary, which they drew from Cervantes, in order to put themselves fully into the role of "such noble knights." By his own judgment, Freud was filled in his youth with a "kind of thirst for knowledge, which, however, was more concerned with human relationships than with natural objects." At that time, a career in law or politics seemed to him a foregone conclusion.

The conversion experience that caused Freud to become a doctor had nothing to do with suffering humanity or with the experience of illness; it occurred in the philosophical realm and was initiated by Goethe's essay on nature.[4] In fact, some of the basic ideas of this essay seem to have been forever melded with Freud's conceptual categories, for example, his preference for "analytical thinking" and his antipathy toward "synthesis,"[5] his honest, lifelong love of "science" and his hatred of any "mysticism,"[6] and finally his enthusiastic support for the idea of not "repressing" any power of the soul in life or in science.[7] How deeply Goethe left his mark on Freud with this essay may well be inferred from the fact that this man, whose work is so filled with quotations from Goethe, to my knowledge never again cited verbatim Goethe's essay on nature but all the more passionately stood for its basic ideas.

The study of medicine must have meant a gigantic disappointment for Freud. The one who at that time knew no other longing
"than that toward philosophical knowledge" had to find out "that
idiosyncrasy and my limited gifts denied me any success in several
scientific disciplines." Perhaps that is why he spent more time with
philosophy than was customary for medical students during his
time. We know for certain that he heard Aristotelian logic from
Brentano, in whose reading seminar he also enrolled, and that he
participated in other philosophical seminars.[8] Finally, the fact that,
upon Brentano's recommendation, the unknown student of medicine was the very one to whom Theodor Gomperz, undisputedly
the best scholar of antiquity in his time, entrusted a volume of his
edition of John Stuart Mill for translation, must have been, in spite
of everything, a proud experience of success for Freud and must
have increased rather than diminished his receptiveness to the content of that volume. Yet what is astonishing is that the decisive
experience of this translation activity was not the encounter with
the social revolutionary Mill—who left Freud completely cold and
even challenged him to opposition[9]—but rather the acquaintance
with Plato, whom Mill admirably interprets in this book.

Mill, who in his essay discusses in detail a work by George Grote,
not only took his translator along into the "school of precise thinking," which he was guaranteed by Plato, but also introduced him to
the basic issues of any text interpretation, with their critical reflection on the question of authenticity, and awakened in him a desire
to tear down prejudices, which was to predominate all his life in
the same way as his antipathy toward Hegel. Plato's veneration of
"truth grounded in reason," with which he challenged his friends to
"unrestrained investigation by means of their own independent
reason," and with which he acknowledged their resulting decisions—whether they agreed with his own views or ran counter to
them—became for Freud the much-cited and often-affirmed model
for interaction with his colleagues within the psychoanalytic
movement. Above all, however, it must have impressed Freud that
Plato, according to Mill, was the first to contemplate the boundary
between the unconscious and conscious activity of the soul[10] and in
the doctrine of reminiscence to describe life as a recollection.[11]
This perception was to reappear in central position in Freud. That

Mill, as well as Grote, expressed his hearty displeasure with Plato's ethical-calculation theory, which allows the "noble light of philosophy" to go out "in a fog of mystical Pythagoreanism," may have had a negative influence on Freud's decision in his disagreement with Wilhelm Fliess.

Plato, whom Freud had come to know through Gomperz also, must have so impressed him that even thirty-three years later he requested a handwritten Plato manuscript of Gomperz's from his widow. For the rest, however, Freud early adopted vis-à-vis philosophers an extremely critical stance, to which we must return later. He would hardly admit that his passionate longing was once for philosophical knowledge.[12] Philosophers were now mentioned only where it was absolutely unavoidable for the support of theory; thus, in the first instance, naturally, there was Darwin, whose teachings at times "powerfully attracted" Freud; then Lamarck, whose developmental ideas he wanted to continue logically with psychoanalysis; G. T. Fechner, to whom had occurred, in his "noble simplicity," the only rational word on dreams; J. F. Herbart, whose mechanistic psychology occasionally served as a point of departure; Theodor Lipps, in whose study he could become absorbed; and Schopenhauer, whom Freud first read in later years when it turned out that he had sailed "unintentionally into the harbor of his philosophy." Freud had forbidden himself the reading of Nietzsche in order not to be hindered by conceptions of expectation. This exhausts the short list of philosophers who through their influence helped to shape psychoanalysis because they impressed and captivated its creator.

Freud's turning-away from philosophy could only have succeeded under the influence of Ernst Brücke, in whose laboratory he found something like a little bit of home; and here he achieved his first notable scientific successes. For Freud, it must have been a kind of asceticism to force his spirit, hungering for philosophical knowledge, into the Procrustean bed of the conceptual categories of natural science that were in vogue at the time in Vienna. They were borne with a strong antiphilosophical affect that remained with Freud for the rest of his life. In Vienna, somewhat later than in Germany, the "battle for liberation" had been carried out against natural philosophy, and now there reigned supreme the orientation in natural science that is associated with the names of Hermann Helmholtz (1821–94), Emil Du Bois-Reymond (1818–96), and Brücke (1819–92). Energetically upheld here was the principle that all manifestations of life are phenomena of the physical world which are moved, according to the principle of the preservation of energy, by the twin forces of attraction and repulsion. Within the human organism too it was held that no forces were operant other than the common physical-chemical ones; if new ones must be assumed, then they must be of like dignity. If one also considers the fact that Theodor Meynert, Freud's teacher after Brücke, energetically held the opinion that psychic phenomena such as volitional occurrences were "nothing but innervational processes from the hemispheres outward," the direction in which Freud's scientific program had to move in the following years becomes clear: localization of psychic processes in the cerebral anatomy and their translation into quantifiable amounts of stimulation. His first scientific publications were in this vein. They finally brought him a lectureship but for many years required of him daily subjection to ever new observations and ever new experiments under the uniformity of research methods. Freud had taken this upon himself with a certain bitterness, as a kind of forced labor, first, because it brought him closer to the goal of being able to establish a family but, second, because he was afraid of his "subjective inclination in scientific research to leave too much to the imagination," as he confessed much later. At this time he wrote to his fiancée, "It's so much nicer to be a human being than a warehouse of certain, uniform experiences." With this he indicated early on his inner leaning away from that inhuman kind of medicine that caused him to become a revolutionary.

Freud turned to regular medical practice not out of an inner motivation but out of the very sober and bitter consideration that as a Jew in a scientific career he would have to wait so long for an assured material existence that he and his fiancée would have grown old in the process. For this reason he finally decided, on the urgent advice of his teachers and friends, to pursue a medical career. Inwardly, however, Freud was not won over to medicine until his encounters with Jean-Martin Charcot, Hippolyte Bernheim, and Josef Breuer.

During 1885–86 Freud had the opportunity, through a travel grant, to work in Paris under Charcot at the famous Salpêtrière hospital. No other person ever had so strong an effect on him; his views and aims were simply turned around. Charcot's lectures left Freud with a quasi-religious feeling of perfection. He had the opportunity to observe hundreds of cases of severe hysteria and became completely familiar with Charcot's method: to observe the same patient again and again until he noticed something new. What Freud assimilated here was a phenomenology of hysteria going into the most minute details, and this assimilation became even more thorough when Charcot entrusted to him the translation of his lectures into German. The phenomenology of hysteria, whose etiology was assumed to lie in the most ordinary traumatic influences, and the operation of hypnosis were the two large areas about which Freud learned something essentially new in Paris. Charcot was interested in the inducement of paralysis by means of hypnosis, because then he could calmly study its various forms and incidentally also enjoy the triumph of making them disappear again through suggestion. Yet he was left standing outside the gates of a real psychological understanding and a psychological therapy. He recognized quite correctly that hysterical symptoms were largely unleashed by the dynamic interaction between the patient and those close to him, but he made no effort to understand these processes; instead, he saw the only cure in the isolation of the patient from his family members and made this the heart of his therapy. This "moral treatment" was expanded only through baths and electrical therapy.

Not much more extensive seemed the therapeutic arsenal with which Freud, after his stay in Paris, opened the medical practice that was now also supposed to serve as the material foundation for his newly established family. It is no wonder that he kept on the lookout for a chance to expand his therapeutic possibilities. He appeared to have found such an opportunity with Bernheim, in Nancy, who in contrast to Charcot applied hypnosis directly as a suggestive means for fighting the symptoms of illness. A few years later, accompanied by a wealthy patient, Freud sought out Bernheim and also translated his work into German. Freud saw his achievement above all in his removing the phenomenon of hypnosis from the realm of the

obscure and bringing it into relationship with the processes of normal psychic life, of waking and sleeping. Suggestion, the leitmotif of
Bernheim's whole work, consists in awakening in another's brain an
"idea that is not tested for its origin but accepted as if it had spontaneously arisen in this brain."

Of the concepts that play a role in Freud's later creative work,
which ones can be traced back to Bernheim and Nancy for their
origin?

1. First, no doubt, was the necessity Freud now clearly saw of
going beyond the formalism of Meynert's anatomy of the brain.[13]

2. Freud adopted from Bernheim as a physician's task the goal of
"influencing . . . the passions and drives, the taste and psychic
abilities of people through suggestion systematically carried out
and skillfully controlled."[14]

3. Bernheim had seen that the "suggestions" of childhood maintain a definite influence on adulthood;[15] and Ambroise-Auguste
Liébault, whom Freud had also met in Nancy, held that it was even
possible that certain psychic behavior models, once they became
established, were inherited from one generation to the next like instincts, so that reason and enlightenment were of little use against
them.[16] Freud was later to discuss very intensively this "archaic heritage" of people.

As meaningful as Freud's encounters with Charcot and Bernheim
were, he owed his actual introduction to practice as a doctor, nevertheless, to his friend and mentor Breuer, to whom we will return
at a later point. Here we have yet to inquire only into the influences
that Freud could possibly have received through his intensive relationship with aesthetic literature.

It is perhaps no accident that during the time of the spiritual
asceticism with which he attempted to hold his imagination in
check in Brücke's and Meynert's laboratories, Freud occupied himself more with *Don Quixote* than with the anatomy of the brain—as
he admitted, shamefaced, to his fiancée. This work reflected not
only the deep sadness of human misery, but in the fellow who
carried out his dreams—however mad they might be—an indict-
ment was also articulated against the sober realities that have lost
their magic. The literature with which Freud otherwise occupied
himself was, to be sure, of a different sort. Goethe and Shakespeare

seem to have been almost totally assimilated. Their quotations are scattered through the whole of Freud's gigantic literary output and bear witness to the familiarity of a loving daily interaction. Almost equally familiar to him were two quite divergent writers, Börne and Heine. At the age of fourteen Freud was given a complete edition of Börne, which he immediately assimilated. It seems to have become his own intellectual property to such an extent that he was astonished when the third page called his attention to the fact that the technique of free association, which he had regarded as his own creation, was already described in great detail by Börne. Heine satisfied Freud's fondness for not always tasteful witticisms,[17] but he must have been especially congenial to Freud because both of them, as Marcuse aptly notes, were "secular with a religious fervor."

Yet as his "actual teachers" Freud named the "writers of the island country, all of them Englishmen and Scots," and for ten years he is supposed to have read nothing but English-language literature. In any case, English was the foreign language he commanded with the least effort and that he most frequently resorted to. In first place here may well be Milton's *Paradise Lost*, which served him over many decades as a book of edification and consolation. It brought to expression the basic idea of overcoming drives and passions through reason, which sows the seeds of morality; this idea must have moved Freud in an unusually strong way and indeed echoes repeatedly as a motif in his works. No less important for Freud may have been the often-mentioned Henry Fielding with his *Tom Jones*. This author, for whom history was everything and who consciously called his output "history" and not a novel or novella, may have contributed to the promotion of Freud's extremely strongly developed historical sense. Going into even human "prehistory," which was later to play so large a role with Freud, was Laurence Sterne with his novel *Tristram Shandy*, which starts with the begetting of the hero, derives everything ab ovo, grants the prenatal existence an extraordinarily large amount of space, and has the hero come into the world only at the end of the third book. The whole work ends with the hero hardly grown out of children's shoes, but in return it pursues all connecting links that develop by tracing spiritual processes with minute exactitude. Yet another impression was made by Dickens's *David Copperfield,* which Freud loved very much. Critical of society but still full of faith in the power of the love of neighbor, it reflects something of the basic attitude to which Freud was certainly closer in old age than in his youth.

A further surprising assertion can be made from Freud's reading: he actually felt himself to be more of a historian than a psychologist. By his own admission, he read substantially more about archaeology than psychology. Especially mentioned are Jacob Burckhardt's *Griechische Kulturgeschichte,* with which he satisfied his fondness for the prehistoric in all human forms; Heinrich Schliemann's *Illias,* in the reading of which he became aware of his love for antiquity as an unfulfilled childhood wish; L. Laistner, by whom he was emphatically directed toward the parallelism of dream and myth ("Die Rätsel der Sphinx"); and finally the Englishman S. E. Baldwin, who conveyed to Freud the theory of the correspondence of ontogeny and phylogeny. As unromantically as Freud may have otherwise always worked, his original point of departure was no doubt the romantic one, with his "overestimation of the beginning" and devotion to the myths of origin. Only through clinical experience did he allow himself, step by step and with effort, to be corrected in this view—as we shall see.

When, in the year 1907, a Viennese bookstore circulated a questionnaire for the ten best books, at the top of Freud's list stood Multatuli, the Dutchman E. D. Dekker, completely unknown to us today. He had not only formulated, with the divine pair Logos and Ananke, the confession of faith in which Freud believed for decades and not until his old age changed into Eros and Ananke, love and reality, but also suggested the motto for the second half of Freud's life: Si vis vitam, para mortem ("If you want life, prepare for death"). He shared with Freud an interest in linguistic history and linguistic development and came up with formulations—which Freud in part adopted word for word—for a more humanitarian sexual ethics, a less repressive character for culture, and a more rational sex education for children. Like Freud, he himself also practiced very little of the sexual freedom that he promoted for others. On Freud's booklist there followed, in a colorful mélange, Kipling, *The Jungle Book;* Anatole France, *Sur la pierre blanche;* Zola, *Fécondité;* Dmitry Sergewitsch Mereschkowski, *Leonardo da Vinci;*

G. Keller, *Die Leute von Seldwyla;* C. F. Meyer, *Huttens letzte Tage;* Macaulay, *Essays;* Gomperz, *Griechische Denker;* and Mark Twain, *Sketches.*

It is significant that no longer on the list is a book that Peter Brückner regards as the key novel for the young Freud, Jens P. Jacobsen's *Niels Lyhne.* As a convinced follower of Darwin, Jacobsen sketches in the novel something like a Werther of unfaith, documenting the tragic, despairing atheism of the nineteenth century. For him, faith in God is flight from raw reality, and he hopes for a time when the earth might become a real home and the stream of love that still climbs toward God might be turned toward neighbor. And yet the hero of the novel does not get rid of faith, because with its powers it seems to have become something like a legacy, deeply buried in the ancient inheritance of the human soul.

There is no doubt that such material must have interested and moved Freud. From it, perhaps, comes a good part of his conception of the unexpected "power" of religion. But the fact that Freud apparently did not remain faithful to this in his mature adult years bears witness to the historical changeability of his thought. It also shows itself in the uneasiness that he repeatedly felt over the images of religion that he had sketched at different stages of development.

The ambivalence that Freud may have felt as a reader also had its fallout in his attitude toward science, which we must now consider, especially in regard to the issue of "ideological suspicion."

FREUD AS SCIENTIST

If we set the question of ideological suspicion directly against Freud's explicit statements on the subject, naturally, we receive a negative answer: No, psychoanalysis is "totally unsuited to form its own ideology." Freud understood as ideology (*Weltanschauung*) an intellectual construction that solves all the problems of our existence uniformly under one superordinated assumption. Psychoanalysis, however, is far from that. It is a psychology of the id, the unconscious, and can therefore only offer in the most diverse areas of knowledge contributions that, at most, might be able to expand previous viewpoints that are based on the ego, on consciousness. What especially made any ideological formation through psychoanalysis seem impossible to Freud was the deep chasm that separated psychoanalysis from every philosophical system. If for philosophers there must first be the main idea under which the details are to be subordinated (one thinks, for example, of Schopenhauer!), for the psychoanalyst the individual observation is primary and he must always be ready to let himself be corrected, modified, and set right. Moreover, Freud confessed openly his personal dislike for the production of ideologies. He believed that one must endure life's journey without such a travel guide that gives information on anything and everything.

Does this admit, therefore, that one can and must distinguish between "psychoanalytic method" and "ideological background," and that for psychoanalysis itself, the ideology with which it is connected makes absolutely no difference? Not at all, in Freud's opinion. He held the production of ideologies to be superfluous, especially because there was already one available that he could recognize and also with which psychoanalysis was supposed to be connected: the scientific world view. On close examination and measured by Freud's own definition, this was actually no ideology at all but rather something like a critical principle: emphasis on the real outer world, acquiescence to truth, rejection of illusion. This view is borne by the conviction that there is no other source of knowledge about the world "than the intellectual processing of carefully tested observations," and it allows no knowledge that is based on revelation, intuition, or divination. In its constant open-endedness and principled correctability, it is capable of unanticipated perfection and represents the one and only way that can lead to the reality of the world outside ourselves.

Is psychoanalysis thus bound thereby to a "rationalistic," positivistic, agnostic, materialistic world view? In my opinion, by no means! Indeed, Freud's deep mistrust of such undertakings consisted ultimately in his concern about a system that could gobble up into one unified monistic formula "all of the beautiful differentiations in nature"[18] and the "contradictions that make life interesting." For him, however, "the magnificence of the world" rested from the very beginning on the "multiplicity of possibilities."[19] Therefore, with Freud, one seeks in vain for clear basic concepts and sharply circumscribed definitions; in his opinion, those are possible only in the intellectual disciplines, and therefore any rapprochement with philosophical metaphysics is carefully avoided. As long as he lived, Freud never rid himself of the suspicion that remnants of the magical approach to reality, which he had observed in children and primitives as faith in the "power of thoughts," had fled into the philosophical systems of the metaphysicians. To them can be traced the illusion that it is possible to produce a consistent picture of the world without any gaps, an illusion that comes into being only through a boundless overestimation of the epistemological worth of our logical operations. Freud considered them presumptuous and cited approvingly Heine's mockery of Hegel: "He stuffs the gaps in the structure of the world with his nightcap and shreds of his dressing gown." What Freud lacked here also was simply respect: "In secret—for, indeed, one may not say it aloud—I believe that metaphysics will just have to be judged a 'nuisance,' a misuse of thinking." His scientific path and his goals were therefore more modestly set. The systematic processing of material did not suit him; the fragmentary nature of his experiences and the sporadic character of his ideas did not permit it. Hence he had to be satisfied with doing research, solving puzzles, and uncovering a little bit of truth.

As clear as Freud's rejection of metaphysics is on the one hand, so clear is it on the other that he intended to allow as the pathway to knowledge only the intellectual processing of carefully tested observations—that is, he wanted to be a scientist. A closer examination reveals, however, that Freud's relationship with science, to which he consciously intended to hold fast all his life, was basically a broken relationship. His own working style could hardly have corresponded to the scientific ideal of his time. He granted to the individual observation far greater significance than was commonly done, and largely scorned the verification of such observations by means of statistically significant and numerically impressive data. The new always came to him "like a brainstorm"; that is, he worked primarily through the intuition he himself despised. Again and again, the writer was for him the enviously observed example of how in the realm of human information one can reach, by "flying," what the scientific viewpoint must achieve while arduously "limping along." Thus he himself finally wrote case histories that to his own amazement read "like novellas."[20]

Freud commented on all the important new discoveries of psychoanalysis with scientifically critical remarks; a line of development can be observed within which, in the struggle between tradition and science, he more and more clearly sided with tradition. As early as 1892, in his memorial to Charcot, he mentioned the idea that the solution of the Middle Ages, which regarded possession by a demon as the cause of hysterical phenomena, seemed to come closer to the truth than contemporary theories. It was only a matter of substituting the scientific terminology of the present for the religious terminology of that dark and superstitious time. After he had devoured the giant mass of scientific literature on dreams, up to Schleiermacher's time, Freud stated that it is the lay conception of the dream, half entangled in superstition, not the medical, scientific view, that comes close to the truth. Later he stressed the close connection between psychoanalytical dream interpretation and the ancient art of interpreting dreams. He became very explicit in the year 1923 when he investigated a seventeenth-century demonic neurosis: "The demonic theories of those dark times have kept their validity in spite of all the somatic conceptions of the 'exact' period of science. These possessions correspond to our neuroses, for whose clarification we again turn to psychic powers."

A little later Freud was already looking back to the "materialistic, or better, mechanistic period" of medicine as something outmoded, although in the beginning he himself had believed in it with great enthusiasm. It had, to be sure, brought magnificent progress to medicine but in the process had still failed in a shortsighted way to appreciate the "most prominent and most difficult among the problems of life," namely, the spiritual phenomena. Now, to be sure, there can be no suggestion at all that Freud ever spoke of an uncritical repristination of the belief in demons. It is a question, rather, of Freud's coming to an ever-stronger recognition that in these mythical conceptual structures something was hidden that is not done and gone but rather is alive in the unconscious of every individual. The more one seeks to deny it and repress it, the more energetically it will come into play in dark ways and penetrate uncontrolled where it is not suspected. Therefore, Freud maintained that it was better to deal consciously with these areas and make them understandable through interpretation. Hence he devoted the last part of his life, from 1923 on, exclusively to the investigation of such cultural and religious phenomena. He described this path expressly as a bit of a "transformation" and regressive development that now allowed him to recognize his life's journey as a "detour through science, medicine, and psychotherapy," leading to what for him was a need from the days of his youth: to understand something of the world's puzzles and to contribute something to their solution. Freud regarded as his "life's triumph" the fact that he had rediscovered in his older years this initial direction of his interest.

Yet it is not only the historical development of his life that makes Freud's relationship with science seem a broken one. There is one area to which Freud repeatedly turned with stubborn persistence, although he could thereby evoke only the puzzled headshaking of his friends. This was the realm of the occult. As a sixty-five-year-old he wrote that if he stood again at the beginning of a scientific career, he would choose no other area of endeavor than this one. He now designated his earlier views as "skeptical, materialistic prejudices" that he could abandon only with difficulty. There is no question that here too Freud did not go over, with flags flying, to the camp of the enemy he had previously fought. His ambivalence seems to be only the keenness of his research genius, which consisted in the fact that he refused to dogmatize results for all time once they had been achieved; he preferred rather to hold them open for the new. Thus he half hoped and half feared that behind occult phenomena—which had reached him primarily in the form of telepathy—might lie something that would lead to the great landslide, a "fearful collapse of critical thinking, of deterministic claims, of mechanistic science, over which all the credulity that has lain ready since the childhood of the human race will rejoice." It is not without a certain maliciousness that Freud paints such a catastrophe, for "psychoanalysis and occultism have experienced the same despicable, arrogant treatment on the part of official science." And so there is no doubt where Freud's sympathies lay and where those of psychoanalysis should lie: "It would not be the first time that it had lent its help to the dark but indestructible premonitions of the people against the scholarly darkness of the educated."

Thus did Freud subject himself to the criticism of having become in his old age "feebleminded, pious, and gullible," and he never stopped promoting the idea that one should be more receptive to the phenomena of telepathy, behind which he presumed an archaic original system of communication by means of direct psychic transfer. When his psychoanalytic friends countered that he might just as well believe in the existence of angels, he explained, undisturbed: "Quite right, and even in God Almighty!"—and that, as far as he was concerned, ended the discussion.

We stand here before a side of the Freudian essence that bears witness to the open-endedness of his thinking but which is hardly rendered correctly with the often-conjured term "skepticism." Certainly Freud was skeptical in the extreme in regard to any unverifiable authority. When he stood for the first time on the Acropolis, he was gripped by a boundless amazement that everything was really the way he had been taught in school. Nevertheless, he rejected for himself the honorary title of philosophical skeptic: "I am no absolute skeptic. Yet of one thing I am quite sure: there are certain things that at present we cannot know." Does such a humble admission not contain more faith than many a pompous conception of God?

One could demonstrate this "other side" of Freud with many other details: for example, with the dimension of depth that could be opened up for him by works of art such as Raphael's *Sistine Madonna*, Titian's *Tribute Money*, or Notre Dame in Paris;[21] or with the thorough confidence of his belief that he had a destiny to fulfill and could not "fall out of the world."[22] Also to be mentioned in this connection is the self-critical clarity with which Freud saw that the application of psychoanalysis to religious phenomena must have the very personal significance of getting them out of one's way, and for this reason he had created a "phantom" for himself "for the purpose of an expeditious, maximally impressive demonstration." Finally, one must also mention here the fact that for the older Freud, love could become an "aim of life completely independent of science."[23]

Certainly these are all individual observations without great cogency. They come down to one common denominator, however, as soon as we try to see them in the context of the fact that probably shaped Freud in the most existential way: that he was a Jew and felt himself one throughout his life.

FREUD AS JEW

Never for a moment, as long as he lived, did Freud fall into the temptation in one way or another to deny his Jewish origin. Although there were times when he felt "something German" stir within him, he had long since decided to suppress this in himself.[24] He would have gladly reduced his connection with Judaism to the simple, concise formula that while he was estranged from the religion of his ancestors, he had never given up the feeling of belonging to his people. Yet how much lay hidden behind that simple formula of the "feeling of belonging" and powerfully forced itself into consciousness as soon as the door was opened! It was not just the things that Freud ascribed to his Jewishness: that he found himself free of the prejudices that restricted others in the use of their intellect, and that he was prepared to side with the opposition and renounce agreement with the "solid majority." It was also not just the fact that he suddenly discovered that whole sections of his written work were conceived and thought out in a decidedly "talmudic" fashion. Nor was it only the knowledge of how intellectual values are to be highly esteemed and how unity can be preserved through ideas; nor indeed, even the awareness of having inherited the total persistence and passion with which his ancestors defended their temple. No, his Jewishness went still deeper; it encompassed his whole personality, his entire soul.[25] Strange and mysterious are the longings that can emerge from this ancestral inheritance, longings for the East, the Mediterranean, "and life of a completely different sort." Dark are the emotional forces that make the attraction of the Jews irresistible and all the more powerful the less they can be put into words, and likewise the clear consciousness of inner identity, the secrecy of the same spiritual makeup.

We pause surprised. So there is a region where words fail, a region that eludes analysis and that one must simply leave alone. After a life of relentless analyses of the most intimate things, which are normally kept to oneself, the eighty-year-old Freud could only call what matters to the Jews "that miraculous thing . . . inaccessible to analysis so far." Now, of course, there was no lack of effort on Freud's part to penetrate the mystery of the Jew, but perhaps we face here again one of those shamefaced admissions that are so easy to overlook in Freud. He was not satisfied with everything he had brought together in terms of intellectual effort and the burden of proof, in order to explain the religious phenomenon. For him it remained "that miraculous thing," still inaccessible to any analysis.

Yet we cannot stop here. Even Freud never fully understood himself in his Jewishness. It remained puzzling to him why he had filled a long life espousing the truth and could not conclude it with an act of denial. "When I ask myself why I have always striven honestly to be considerate of the other person and perhaps charitable, and why I do not give it up when I notice that it is harmful, then, of course, I have no answer." Could it not be that Freud himself had carefully hidden his own faith? May we not, and must we not, therefore, venture the effort to understand him a little better than he understood himself? He showed, as no other, that one cannot understand oneself without the so-called objective, nor so-called objects without oneself. May we, therefore, take what Freud has left us in the way of an interaction with religion and also question it in regard to the character of his subjective faith, even though Freud himself sought carefully to hide this very aspect? We would like to attempt this from three points of departure: from his relationship with Hasidism, then from his work on Michelangelo's *Moses,* and finally from his writing on *Der Mann Moses und die monotheistische Religion* (Moses and monotheism [three essays]).

Freud's father came from a Hasidic milieu. Except for one letter, Freud always left this fact unmentioned. Yet it might have contributed in an essential way to the fact that on the occasion of a highly casual and almost scurrilous encounter with his Hasidic inheritance, Freud felt himself deeply stirred and addressed. In any case, he thought it necessary to capture this entire experience in more polished form and to turn over to his fiancée his long and curious "letter" about it. From 16 July to 27 July 1882, Freud visited his fiancée in Wandsbek. One day he went to Hamburg to have stationery printed with the initials of Martha and Sigmund, thereby reserving it for the exclusive use of the two lovers. The proprietor to whom Freud happened to go proved to be a pupil of Martha's grandfather, Isaac Bernays (1792–1849), who was the head of the Sephardic congregation in Hamburg. This old man presented to him a picture of his faith, which of course was not new to Freud, since he was familiar with such things because of his father, but which nonetheless moved him very deeply. What were the individual traits of this Judaism that he felt were especially worth mentioning to his fiancée?

First, religion is seen here no longer from the viewpoint of rigid dogma but from that of meaningfulness. What humankind has believed for centuries, so it is argued here, cannot be nonsense; it must have a meaning. This consists not in the fact that religion exists as something holy but in the fact that one can rejoice in this deep meaning that is found in religion. It stands open to criticism and can become the object of reflection, of refined artistic taste, and of increased logical requirements. On the other hand, one can speak of pleasure here completely without embarrassment. The Jew was created for pleasure, and he should celebrate every little pleasure: the Jew is for joy, and joy is for the Jew. Finally, out of this form of piety is brought to expression the idea that any ethical sacrifice is possible only on the basis of love and through love. Religion as the finding of meaning, as challenge to pleasure and joy, and as ethics on the basis of the love motive—that is what Freud set forth here and what caused him to pledge, "Even if the form in which the old Jew felt at home no longer offers us any shelter, something of the heart, the essence of meaningful and joyous Judaism, will not leave our house."

We may also point to a further small trait of this experience that may not be entirely unimportant. Again and again it has been asked why, when dealing with the question of the therapeutic goal of psychoanalytic treatment, Freud with stubborn persistence repeatedly quoted the formula—felt as understatement and in many ways made ridiculous—that he had to be satisfied with reestablishing for his patients a little capacity for work and pleasure. In reading the report of the meeting with that old Jew—whom Freud estimated to be fifty-four and who in reality was twenty years older—one learns that it was the old man's formula, with which he sought to summarize inner and outer well-being. Shortly thereafter the expression was adopted by Martha, was employed and verified by Freud, and then disappeared many years only to be used again when it was a question of conjuring up the condition of spiritual health. What was conjured up, however, was the picture of that happy old Jew who understood how to live a form of piety that could even impress Freud!

In February 1914 there appeared in the psychoanalytical journal *Imago* an anonymous article with the following footnote:

> The editors did not deny acceptance to this contribution, which, strictly speaking, does not conform to our purposes, because the author, who is known to us, stands close to analytical circles and because his way of thinking shows, nonetheless, a certain similarity with the method of psychoanalysis.

The title was "Der Moses des Michelangelo" (The Moses of Michelangelo). The secret of the author's identity was not revealed until ten years later: the article came from Freud. It was the only time that Freud published a work anonymously; the reasons given for this procedure, which even the closest colleagues could not understand, were highly transparent. That is, apparently concealed in this work was something of that most intimate thing about which Freud otherwise remained closemouthed. Twenty years after the appearance of the article, he described his relationship to it as that to a "love child." For three weeks Freud stood daily before Michelangelo's statue of Moses in San Pietro in Vincoli in Rome, in part because it held such an unusually strong fascination for him, in part because he wanted very much to find out why it could have such a powerful effect.[26] In the article in question, we discover Freud's interpretation. Yet why the work of art made such a strong impression on Freud and why that impression had to be so carefully concealed—these are questions that only a depth-psychological interpretation of the article can answer.

Freud's interpretation of Michelangelo's *Moses* is not sensational. Previously it had been generally assumed that the artist wanted to capture here the moment in which Moses, coming down from the mountain, saw the golden calf and, full of rage, was on the verge of shattering the tablets of the law. Supported by innumerable tiny details that he had observed and amassed with loving care, Freud was able to show that Michelangelo had another Moses in mind: in the statue he wanted to capture not the imminent outbreak of wrath but a Moses who has overcome his passions. "Moses will now remain thus in subdued rage, in pain mixed with contempt. He remembered his mission, and for its sake he forwent the satisfaction of his emotion." Freud's summarizing judgment reads, "Moses becomes the bodily expression of the highest psychic achievement that is possible for a human being, the overpowering of one's own passions in favor of and in fulfillment of a destiny to which one has committed oneself."

Freud's work on Moses should be granted, therefore, the rank of an aesthetic hermeneutic, above all because in wonderful clarity it brings to expression how the object of observation and the observer are here linked together in the hermeneutical circle. It takes no great effort to discover in Freud's work the scientific and autobiographical contexts of his magnificent interpretation of Moses: "When the ego brings to the superego the sacrifice of an instinct denial, it expects as a reward to be more loved by the superego. It feels as pride the consciousness of deserving this love." Also to be cited at this point is an excerpt from a letter to J. J. Putnam:

> You see, I must tell you . . . that I consider myself a very moral person, who can endorse that good dictum of Th. Vischer: Morality is always self-evident. I believe that in a sense of right and consideration for neighbor, in displeasure at causing others to suffer or taking advantage of them, I can match the best people I have met. Actually, I have never done anything common or malicious and feel no temptation to do so, either.

For Freud—as the one who identified with the Moses who overpowers the passion in his own breast in favor of the destiny to which he has pledged and committed himself—this seems to work smoothly, and one is struck by many other places in his total work that seem to support it. Here we add but two especially characteristic statements: "All such progress in spirituality has the result of increasing the self-esteem of the person, of making one proud, so that one feels superior to others who remain under the spell of sensuality." And an excerpt from a letter to his fiancée concerning a production of *Carmen* in Paris:

> The riffraff live it up, and we do without. We do without in order to maintain our integrity; we are frugal with our health, with our enjoyment, with our emotions; we save ourselves for something—for what, we ourselves don't know—and this habit of constantly suppressing natural instincts gives us the character of refinement.

Thus the work of art and its interpreter are most certainly linked together in a complete and convincing circle. We have only to ask ourselves why Freud had to be so careful to conceal the proud feeling of "cultural progress through the domination of instinct," through which he could identify with so powerful a figure as that of Moses. If we turn again to the text of Freud's interpretation, we notice that in addition to containing the apparent identification with the Moses figure, it also contains another, less emphasized trait: ". . . as if I myself belonged to the riffraff on which his eye is fixed, which hold to no conviction, which do not want to wait and trust and rejoice when they have received again the illusion of the graven image." Thus one can see it also from this angle: Freud is not only the Moses who seeks to lead the riffraff into the promised land of instinct denial but is also one of the riffraff, one who is going astray from his destiny, who has no trust, who wants to have everything right now, and who secretly (perhaps by means of occultism or telepathy?) still builds himself graven images. It is one of the very few places where Freud is able to connect the phenomenon of guilt to himself.[27] Yet perhaps this is the most profound reason that Michelangelo's *Moses* could clarify for him the mystery of his existence as a Jew only in an imperfect way.

Freud seems to be possessed by the Moses problem and a second time attempted a new exposition of Jewish existence, this time based not on a work of art but on appropriate biblical sources. It strikes one as much less proud and self-conscious. This time it is not surrounded by a veil of mystery, and Freud even confessed candidly to various correspondents that he actually wrote it only out of personal motivation. It "would not let go of his imagination" and tormented him "like an unredeemed spirit." Neither did the work's historical foundation seem to him certain enough, nor did it please him especially well; nevertheless, it was enough for him that he himself could believe in the solution to the problem, because it had pursued him throughout his whole life. The publication was delayed at first because Freud did not want to offend the Catholic church, which at the time still served as a bulwark against the National Socialist barbarism.

Where lies the solution to the problem that pursued Freud

throughout his life? Fascinated by the technique of source separation, with which he first became acquainted while researching his second work on Moses, Freud separated Moses into two historical figures: a less important, primitive, and violent Midianite Moses, who served the fire demon Yahweh, and the "actual" Moses, who was no Jew at all but rather a prominent Egyptian, who represented the highly spiritual, monotheistic Aton religion and who adopted, as it were, the wretched enslaved Jewish people, led them out of captivity, and pledged them to monotheism. This time it is no longer the feeling of moral excellence that aids immediate understanding, but the question of the basic feeling of an election and acceptance that runs like a common thread through the whole work. Its focus is the shaping of the character of the people through the rejection of magic and mysticism, through stimulation to progress in spirituality, and through the demand for sublimations, and it is also the way "the people, overjoyed by the possession of the truth and overcome by the consciousness of election, achieved a high estimation of the intellectual and an emphasis on the ethical." To be sure, that stubborn people killed its leader and since then, in spite of all its magnificent achievements, must wander through history with the stigma of a guilt feeling in the soul.

The extent to which one can read the article on Moses autobiographically in regard to Freud certainly raises for researchers many more important questions. For our purposes it is important merely to draw connecting lines between the man Freud, his spiritual roots, and the work itself, and thus to refute some of the objections that have been raised from the theological side against dealing with Freud. Now we must turn our attention to the work itself.

3

THE THEORY

Points of Departure and Disagreements

Freud's findings were drawn from three sources especially: from daily observation and therapeutic interaction with his patients, from dialogue and interchange with trusted friends, and from disagreements with opponents. Freud himself felt it to be "neurotic" that an intimate friend and a hated enemy were always necessary requirements of his emotional life, and that relatively often both emotional attitudes developed one after the other in regard to the same person. He held early childhood experiences responsible for this.[1] As Freud himself learned with pronounced astonishment, he could hate for intellectual reasons. Therefore, in those of his intimate friends who later became hated enemies, it is very easy to see representatives of the thought patterns and convictions toward which Freud himself inclined for a time but from which he then freed himself; he knew how to block any return to them by rejecting earlier valued friends in order thus to clear the way for his own creative ideas.

It is therefore fruitful to develop the actually new things found and processed by Freud out of his respective disagreements with the opponents who were once his friends. Hence, in the following, there can certainly be no question of an objective and proper evaluation of the scientific achievements of these men. We will get to know them only through Freud's glasses and only in their function as catalysts, as it were, for Freud's development. The abruptness with which Freud turned away from them once the decision against them had been made was not based only on his character. It also had an objective basis in the fact that it was Freud's practice always to exhibit an especially great responsibility vis-à-vis his "object of knowledge," because in him theoretical views and therapeutic treatment were so intimately related to each other. Since it was always a matter of living persons and not just abstract ideas, the threshold of tolerance for deviations could only be low. This may also be the reason why the differences of opinion between various psychotherapeutic schools were settled with the same seriousness and the same passion that we are otherwise familiar with only in theological discussions. Of course, here too, as well as there, the tendency toward strong language is greatest when one understands the least, and indeed, Freud himself in his interaction with Oskar Pfister gave a fine example of how people can exchange truths and crudities yet remain good friends.

BREUER AND SEXUALITY

Without doubt Dr. Josef Breuer (1842–1925) was the mentor to whom Freud largely owed his introduction to independently conducted medical activity and the building-up of his own practice. When Freud opened his office, Breuer, who was almost fifteen years older, not only had behind him a considerable scientific career in Ernst Brücke's laboratory but had also built up an extensive celebrity practice for the sake of which he had given up science. His economic situation allowed him to support Freud financially in the latter's unusually difficult beginning years. Like Freud he had brought into his practice as intellectual equipment the physiological foundation of medicine in the sense of Hermann Helmholtz and Brücke. Yet this showed him ever more clearly what Freud had already noticed in his first patients: that one finally works not with one's method but with one's personality. How physiologically defined science could be reconciled with the psychological experience of practice was the problem that brought Breuer and Freud together and the problem whose solution they worked toward together during several years of common research and reflection.

The area that seemed most favorable for such a purpose was that of hysteria, which Freud had studied with Jean-Martin Charcot, and the means that might be applied was hypnosis. Breuer had an extraordinary stroke of luck to present: a young woman who became ill with a case of hysteria that could be termed nothing short of classic. Moreover, she was so highly intelligent that she herself largely prompted and suggested the new means of therapy that Breuer followed with her. Although Freud himself never met this patient, who was to become famous as Anna O., he was so fascinated by Breuer's notes on the case that he suggested a joint publication with several other observations on hysteria. The theoretical concept that was agreed upon traced the hysteria back to an abnormal excitability of the nervous system, with the symptoms being regarded as the products of excess energy for which there was no other application.

In this joint effort the partners found themselves still operating very much on the basis of Brücke's physiological point of departure, with the ideal of the measurability of all processes, and they hoped to take the psychic traumas, which had a pathogenic effect perhaps leading finally to a kind of "consciousness splitting," and make them comprehensible as quantitative shifts in amounts of psychic energy. Yet when Freud on the basis of further observations came upon the idea that those mysterious "quantities of energy" that can cause hysterical symptoms could be of a sexual nature, that is, a libido shoved aside from its proper application, Breuer became noticeably uncomfortable and withdrew from the still-new partnership by taking back his agreement to a joint publication. Only after Breuer's death did Freud uncover the true reasons for this sensitivity. That is, the case of Anna O., after a very satisfactory initial course of therapy, had a postlude that was extremely confusing to Breuer. On the evening of the day in which all her symptoms had been overcome, he was called to her again and found her confused and bent over with cramps in the lower abdomen. When asked what was the matter, she gave as an answer: Now the baby that Dr. B. gave me is coming. Freud added laconically, "In conventional horror, he took flight and turned the patient over to a colleague."

Freud tried in vain to convince Breuer that the erotic powers breaking forth here must be researched just like all the other phenomena of hysteria, but his emotional aversion to this area persisted. In Freud's opinion, Breuer's self-confidence and his resistance to criticism were not on the same plane as the rest of his intellectual development. Finally he promised his cooperation on the "studies" only on the condition that all sexual questions were to remain in the background. We would certainly do Breuer an injustice if we were to see as the single motive for his rejection of Freud's sexual theories a narrow moralistic prejudice and the fear of criticism from colleagues. His doubts were substantially deeper and had to do with his basic scientific convictions. Even in the events of psychic illness he could acknowledge only impersonal "forces" that could be reduced to physiological quantification. Freud, who also saw erotic forces at work in the doctor-patient relationship, advanced much more strongly into the "personal" area. Above all, he believed he felt in the behavior of the patient toward the doctor a defense behind which the actual pathogenic experiences were concealed. Breuer, on the other hand, saw in that behavior, which he also observed, no personal factors but tried instead to objectify it as "hypnoid conditions," an idea that Freud later called "unfortunate, superfluous, and irrelevant." How much Breuer vacillated between his personal inclination toward Freud and his basic scientific position is best seen in the fact that he passionately and warmly took Freud under his protection in the society of physicians but afterwards told him in private, "I still don't believe it." For the final break with this man, whom he personally esteemed so highly, Freud placed particular responsibility on the fact that Breuer remained committed to a more physiological theory whereas Freud in his sexual theory moved further and further away from physiology and turned to actual psychological categories.

Even Freud still hoped for a time to be able to support his sexual theories in a physiological-chemical fashion, but then he developed them in a kind of venturous defiance and in clear opposition to Breuer's basic position. Freud's views especially proved their fruitfulness when he applied to sexuality one category that was completely foreign to physiology, namely, that regarding the question of history. The application of the historical perspective to sexuality (1) allowed one to inquire for the first time about the genesis of sexuality, (2) described its various stages of maturation, and (3) endeavored to clarify the question of instinct destiny.

The question of genesis entered psychology through romanticism and found its high point in Carl Gustav Carus's historical views on the soul.[2] These historical reflections had not been applied to sexual matters before the time of Freud, and Freud himself was the first one who relentlessly raised the question of the genesis of sexuality. On the basis of the observations he had been able to make with his patients, and through penetrating metapsychological reflections, he brought about an entirely new interpretation of what was understood as sexuality. The starting point for his observations is the two-stage onset of sexual development, that is, the astonishing observation that humans are the only living beings in nature in which sexual development proceeds in two temporally separated developmental thrusts. In early childhood one can observe an immature but clearly sexually tinted stage of instinctual development, which is replaced by a latent period, after which prepuberty and puberty bring a second edition, as it were, of early childhood sexual development with the physiological maturation of sexuality. As the first stage of this sexual development Freud observed the path from mother-child symbiosis to what he called autoeroticism. Out of the stage of the newborn's total dependence on the mother, the child finds a certain independence through the pleasurable concentration on the organs of its own body. Since one can observe in the small child a pleasurable occupation with its own body parts, which is by no means limited to the genitals, Freud called this phase the polymorphously perverse stage, a time in which the organization of the pleasurable occupation of the organism moves forward through definite, precisely determinable phases. A phase of orality is to be observed in which the rhythmic stimulation of the mucous membrane of the mouth stands in the foreground of interest; in the anal phase, the functions of elimination and their products can be entirely objects of gratification; then in the phallic phase interest in the male genitalia and their possible symbolic representation stands in the foreground, even in little girls.

Through the observation and description of these various developmental stages, psychoanalysis, for the first time in human history, saw itself in a position to illuminate satisfactorily the origin of so-called sexual perversions, which had always been explained previously as phenomena of degeneration. Sexual perversions are thus nothing but an arrested development or a reversion to an infantile stage of sexuality, for it is the destiny of sexuality to grow out of this autoerotic, narcissistic stage and arrive at a transference of the libido to other objects. Through the assumption of an object relationship that comes about by way of libidinous fixation, the ego libido gradually becomes the object libido. Childhood development evolves into the famous Oedipus situation, in which the mother represents to the little boy the first affectionately desired love object whereas the father is felt as a rival; for the little girl, the situation is reversed. In every childhood upbringing one can observe the phase in which the little boy has a decidedly good relationship with his mother yet a tense relationship with the father, while the girl gets along better with the father and falls into a pronounced crisis in her relationship with her mother. This classical Oedipal situation is normally resolved by the child through identification; that is, the boy overcomes the hopelessly superior father, or the girl the hopelessly superior mother, who stands in the way of a realization of affectionate desires toward the love object, by assuming the father or mother into the child's own ego, into the child's own person. Demands and wishes that are presented to the child by the father or mother or some other guardian are therefore introjected into their own level in the ego, the so-called superego. Here the foundation is laid for any later formation of conscience. The origins of sexuality can, therefore, be traced very clearly from the stage of mother-child symbiosis into the stage of autoeroticism and its various phases, through the first object relationship and Oedipal situation, and right up to the time of identification with the parent of the same sex.

Now, after this first step of the genetic development of sexuality comes the task of the maturation of sexuality. When we speak in this connection of maturation, we are not referring to physiological maturation, that is, to the ability to generate reproductive cells, which in our present civilization, indeed, occurs very early in the life of a growing individual. In the psychological sense, maturation of sexuality means something fundamentally different, namely, the process that Freud expressed in the classic formulation "from pleasure principle to reality principle." In the early phase of sexual development, the small child makes an attempt to live unrestrictedly in accordance with the pleasure principle; it has the idea that the surrounding world is there only to serve the satisfaction of its own needs. Almost from the first day of life, however, the child must also learn to adapt itself to reality and to integrate this reality into its inner life through acts of denial. On this road to the reality principle the child must now also sacrifice pleasurable occupation with its own body (which psychoanalysis has named forepleasure) to a higher goal, namely, the concentration of sexual feelings on the genitals and on the concomitant submission of the sexual function to the service of reproduction.

Maturation of sexuality in the psychological sense consists in the necessary integration of the partial drives into a new and larger whole, namely, mature sexuality. In it the partial drives are held together by the bond of personal love and thus cannot become absolute or independent, as happens in sexual perversion.

The application of the historical viewpoint to sexuality also means, however, that henceforth the fate, the destiny, the vicissitudes of instincts and drives will be investigated; it means that—as opposed to a static psychology of ability—the nature of instinct will be transformed into a dynamic movement of destiny. There are four instinct destinies upon which Freud especially focused his attention. The *first* is the complete reversal, which has, of course, a double sense: one in the antithesis of active and passive, and a second in the antithesis of a reversal with regard to content, in the sense of a voyeurism that is expanded through exhibitionism. A *second* instinct destiny is a turning toward oneself, which can be observed in normal childhood development on the level of narcissism. One sees, naturally, that the way to the reality principle is repeatedly threatened by such a regression to the level of narcissism. A *third* instinct destiny is repression, which occurs when the conceptual representation of the instinct is completely removed and banned from consciousness by the instinct impulse so that the instinct stimulus as such can never become conscious at all. The instinct stimulus, however, does not disappear; it is only pushed down into the realm of the unconscious, where it can solidify into complexes, bind psychic forces, and finally come to light again in a completely different place, wearing the clothing of neurotic symptoms. Finally, the *fourth* instinct destiny that Freud describes is sublimation. In contrast to repression, the instinct stimulus is here accepted by the ego, that is, taken into cognizance. Now repudiation appears in place of repression. The instinctive desire is not granted immediate satisfaction, but the energy bound to it brings satisfaction on another level so that it can make itself felt creatively in the life of the individual.

Now, this historically oriented, genetic description of sexuality is also consistent with the historical-philosophical interpretation attempted by psychoanalysis. Beginning with the basic principle, still unrefuted in our day, that phylogeny apparently corresponds to ontogeny, Freud saw himself in a position to describe the historical process on the analogy of the personal developmental process. In this way the force shaping that history can be seen from the standpoint of the return of the repressed. Starting with the observation that repressed instinct stimuli in the personal life of an individual have an ominous tendency to reappear in deformed and distorted ways, one can also interpret the historical process as such a process of the reappearance of the repressed. Thus in regard to sexuality, antiquity could be designated the early-childhood stage of polymorphous perversity. The time in which Greek metaphysics ruled the West would then be the latent period, in which it really succeeded for centuries in preventing conscious interaction with sexuality, so that finally it falls the lot of the present time to arrange a conscious interaction with sexuality and the mature integration of the various instinctive tendencies. This is an observation that stands in remarkable agreement with other historical-philosophical interpretations of our time.

FLIESS AND THE BODY-SOUL PROBLEM

Disappointed by Breuer, Freud fell almost head over heels into a new friendship, although most biographers do not understand what could have been the bond. Freud came to know and value Dr. Wilhelm Fliess (1858–1928) on the occasion of a period of university study that Fliess completed in Vienna. For over a decade he was the only one with whom Freud could carry on a scientific exchange, his only public, as he liked to call Fliess in imitation of a humorous phrase from Nestroy. Freud esteemed him unusually highly, felt himself at times far inferior to him, and with effort drew from this friend's recognition some self-confidence.[3] Fliess, who lived in Berlin, was likewise a follower of the Helmholtz school; indeed, he tried to absolutize one of its aspects and maintained that in the end medical science must express its results in mathematical language. Thus he developed a theory of periodicity according to which every significant experience in human life was defined deterministically through numerical values. Freud let himself be influenced by this representative of esoteric number games in a way that is hard to understand today, perhaps precisely because to Freud, who was turning ever more to linguistic communication and its consequences, this world seemed so infinitely far, foreign, and fascinating.

Above all, it must have had a liberating effect on Freud finally to find someone with whom he could discuss in a completely objective way the question of sexuality that occupied him so much. Fliess showed a special interest in this problem. With great fervor he supported the idea of human bisexuality and suggested to Freud the idea that what is repressed is the nature of the opposite sex, which is present in every person. Thus Fliess had in mind totally sexualizing repression and basing it on biology instead of psychology, and to this end he offered a series of sexual-chemical hypotheses that at first were able to get a real hold on Freud. In his enthusiasm over the fact that Fliess was free of prejudgments in regard to sexuality, he obviously did not notice that Fliess was trying to bind him with the chains of physiology even more strongly than Breuer did—namely, by urging him to integrate the whole of psychology and brain physiology. Freud made similar sketches—although later he never again showed any interest in these manuscripts—in which, among other things, he made an attempt to produce a psychology defined by natural science, "that is, to represent psychic processes as the quantitatively determined conditions of demonstrable material parts." But his mechanical enlightenment of psychological problems was not successful. Only for a moment could he give himself to the illusion that "everything seems to work together, the gears fit together, and one gets the impression that the thing really is a machine and soon will even run by itself."

Yet after a short time Freud became certain that he could go no further in this direction and that he could expect from it no solution to the puzzle of human life. Almost with a bad conscience, he moved more and more away from the working methods of his friend, but he sought to maintain the friendship by suggesting a kind of division of labor. In his own way, Fliess was to enlighten Freud on the physiological mechanism of his clinical findings. Indeed, Freud expressed the hope of finding with Fliess the basis on which he could stop explaining psychologically, in order "to undergird physiologically" again. He went so far into the territory of his friend that the two discussed seriously whether migraines could be evoked through a toxic effect that was caused by the insufficient elimination of the "sexual stimulating substance."

Although Fliess's calculations and numerical games became ever more complicated and artificial, Freud assured his friend that he had no reservations concerning Fliess's "periods." Nevertheless, the intellectual alienation was not endurable. Freud's descriptions of the "division of labor" show how deeply and fundamentally the two dissimilar friends were separated: "you the biological, I the psychological"; "you at the end of the stars, I at the end of the soul"; "you with the brightness of the sun, I with the darkness of the unconscious." These pictures show that here two basically different forms of thinking were thrown together: Fliess was pledged to numbers and therefore had to design abstract systems; Freud was committed to language and therefore had to remain with reality. Soon Freud confessed to his friend that he comprehended nothing of his communications, although he had opened all sensory ports and had never before faced Fliess with so much dumb expectancy. He lamented that unfortunately he had very little participation in Fliess's work and progress and was scarcely in a position to follow his "beautiful explanations"; he placed the blame on the fact that their ideas and inclinations did not go in the same direction and finally stated with resignation that they had fallen away from each other by quite a bit. Yet Freud saw himself subjected to massive criticism from Fliess when Freud took sides with tradition against science, and Fliess asserted that Freud's whole primitive history of hysteria had already been known and publicized a hundred times—to be sure, several centuries ago. "I have always said that the theories of the Middle Ages and of the ecclesiastical courts on being possessed are identical with our foreign-body theory and the division of consciousness." Yet Fliess could find no enjoyment at all in the Middle Ages, and just as little when Freud suddenly gathered a collection of profound Jewish stories and even began to take an interest in myths—and as the latest product of his intellectual labor, presented a psychomythology!

The misunderstanding that was finally to break the bond of friendship shows all too clearly the direction in which Freud had developed in the meantime. His patients had long ceased to be the objects of attempts at scientific explanation and therapy; his central concern was rather to understand them. Other people can be understood, however, only to the extent that one has understood oneself, and this brought Freud to his own self-analysis, which he tried to push forward with enormous energy. The circular structure of the understanding process and the reciprocity of the personal relationship in the therapeutic situation were already so much a part of the indispensable center of his thinking that it had to mean the end of their friendship when Fliess answered Freud's efforts in this direction with the reproach that he was a "mind reader" who read his own thoughts into others and that his interpretations meant nothing more than the projection of his own feelings. Thus Freud made the final break: "You know that I have no trace of quantitative talent and no memory for figures and amounts . . . and you are also no longer my public." With this final separation Freud secured psychoanalysis from the influence of a man whom his Berlin colleagues called a "numbers player, inexperienced in the simplest principles of arithmetic" and "a numbers mystic who belongs at the end of the Middle Ages." In retrospect, Freud himself could only say that it would have been a "misfortune" if he had subjected psychoanalysis to Fliess's sexual biology.

Without doubt, the Fliess epoch was the time in Freud's life when he developed his scientific independence; here lie the decisive points of departure for his whole work. Let us briefly recall, therefore, some of the stops along this section of Freud's developmental path, which was certainly not easy for him:

1. Already in his "preanalytical" writing on aphasia, which is, unjustly, little known, Freud protested against the confusion of physiological and psychological facts. He expressed doubts "about the correctness of a model that essentially rests on localization," according to which Theodor Meynert in particular held that

thoughts and memories are bound to certain brain centers. Freud energetically set himself against the assumption of a causal relationship between physiological and psychic processes. It was important to him to demonstrate that the physiological equivalents of psychic activity are not something at rest in the brain that can be localized there but rather have the nature of a process. Here already the dynamic, eventful character of everything psychic is placed in the foreground in opposition to the static viewpoint of a psychology of ability.[4] In a clarity deserving of thanks, he corrected the previous conception that a "symbolic" relationship exists between object and object concept by saying that one can at most speak of such a symbolic relationship between word concept and object concept, and he created thereby an important presupposition for later possibilities of linguistic understanding.[5]

2. At the moment when Freud began to ask about meaning, he turned away finally from the conceptual path marked by natural science and physiology. The discovery of meaning occurs through the process of interpretation. In the case of symptoms, this meant going back to early childhood traumas. At first he credited as traumatic only sexual seductions that had actually taken place. Gradually, however, he came to accord traumatic effects to fantasies and thus to grant a rightful place to the "psychic reality beside the practical." In the case of a dream, this means "replacing it with something that fits in as a full-fledged, homogeneous link in the chain of our spiritual actions." In the case of myth, it means, in spite of all distortions and misunderstandings, seeing represented there the reality of the past by nullifying the effective powers of these distortions. Instead of isolated organs, the person as a whole gradually comes again to the fore, including of course his manifestations. Not only was physiology transformed into psychology of the unconscious; the effort was also undertaken "to change metaphysics into metapsychology."

3. In that moment when Freud required self-analysis as the absolute prerequisite to any analysis of others, "objective" science's direct path to knowledge was abandoned. Into its place moved the circular structure: I can analyze others only by means of the experience I have gained myself, and I can analyze myself only with objectively gained knowledge. In this way Freud discovered love of

mother and jealousy of father even in himself—and understood all at once the gripping power of King Oedipus. On the other side, the great mythic motifs now could also help him to understand his patients better. Already during the early years of his friendship with Fliess there dawned on him something like a "world formula"— that he would one day reduce the whole of human existence to the common denominator of the struggle between destruction and love: "Everything surges and glimmers, an intellectual hell, one layer behind another; in the darkest core the outline of Lucifer-Amor is visible."

Understanding thus became central. That this means, however, always to understand better than one understands oneself—this did not occur to him until his friendship with Lou Andreas-Salomé, whom he called "an understander par excellence" because she always understood things better than they were presented to her, and because she always understood more than was there.[6]

4. As a particularly clear sign of the transformation that occurred in Freud in regard to the body-soul problem, one must consider his theories on anxiety, which reflect the changes in the liveliest way. At first Freud sought the source of anxiety not in the psychic realm but in a psychic element of sexual life. When abundant physical sexual tension arises but cannot become emotion through psychic processing, it is transformed into anxiety. Thus anxiety is nothing other than libido diverted away from its application. Freud considered repression above all to be the cause of the corresponding processes, yet he soon noticed that he was thereby regarding anxiety in a way that was too undifferentiated. Therefore, he adopted the distinction, in use since Kierkegaard, between anxiety and fear: "Anxiety is related to the condition and disregards the object; fear directs attention directly to the object." Fear is thus a sensible signal in service of the instinct toward self-preservation, which is supposed to initiate the flight reflex; anxiety must appear senseless and can perhaps be designated anxiety in the face of nothingness.

Now, just as he had accorded traumatizing power to fantasy, Freud decided here to grant to internal reality the same dignity as to external: he applied the fear mechanism also to anxiety. The source of anxiety is then to be sought no longer in external but rather in internal reality. Anxiety thus becomes a signal that is supposed to initiate repression, for repression corresponds to a "flight attempt of the ego in the face of the libido, which is felt as danger."

With this, however, the last remnants of the old physiological theories were abandoned. Neither through physical energy nor through chemistry can anxiety be explained; it is possible only in personal categories: "The ego is the actual location of anxiety. . . . It develops the flight reflex by retracting its own possession of the threatening perception or the similarly regarded process in the id (repression) and turning it into anxiety."[7] Thus repression does not create anxiety; rather, anxiety creates repression. It is the strongest indication of human vulnerability in general, for the danger situation is the "recognized, remembered, and expected situation of helplessness." It gives eloquent testimony to the basic feeling of human impotence and abandonment. Of course, it can be better "understood" from the situation of a little child, but overcoming it represents a lifelong task. It is a sign "that communication with fellow human beings has lost its immediacy." Therefore, Gustav Bally saw in Freud's theory of anxiety a profound indication of human nature itself. The anxiety that leads to repression is experienced as unknown, threatening abundance, because "in the moment when familiar contemporary structures are lost, there are aroused possibilities of an original kind that are not accepted in the plan of existence that is valid in a group." Being alone means for the "weak ego" a changed world structure to which a person is not equal without interpretation. Thus, the way of the anxiety theories leads out of the narrowness of the conceptual constrictions of physical science and into the breadth of a horizon on which human reality as a whole can come to expression.[8]

ADLER AND INSTINCT THEORY

While for years Fliess was regarded in Freud's imagination as the superior partner, Alfred Adler (1870–1937) belonged among the first disciples who gradually gathered around Freud at the beginning of the new century and whom he brought together for discussion and exchange in the "Wednesday Psychological Society." Adler seems to have been the one among the disciples who demonstrated the most independent thinking and the strongest leadership qualities. Freud soon made him president of the slowly growing Viennese organization and hoped to be able to step more and more into the background. Yet with Adler there developed for Freud something like a little "Fliess redivivus." What Adler attempted to do with psychoanalysis caused Freud to return very quickly to the scene in order to try to intervene with corrections in many discussions, until the breaking point was reached: together with nine followers—all socialists—Adler withdrew from the Vienna group with the remark that he had no desire to live his whole life in Freud's shadow.

With Adler, Freud encountered for the first time the nightmare of the "system." What Freud's psychoanalysis carefully avoided— namely, making the claim of providing a complete theory of human spiritual life in general—was Adler's aim from the very beginning. What psychoanalysis had often enough been unjustifiably reproached for actually held true, in Freud's opinion, in the case of Adler: he wanted "to make human behavior and character understandable with the same grasp as neurotic and psychotic illnesses themselves." That would not work, however, without very considerable reductionist tendencies in regard to psychoanalysis. By this "system thinking" Freud meant Adler's main idea, which, in Freud's opinion, was gained from a prejudgment; it comes from an individual's self-assertion, from his will to power, which as "masculine protest" makes itself known in the same way both in life style and in character formation and neurosis. With that the stress falls one-sidedly on the ego instincts, which Adler so strongly emphasized that in the end he completely denied libidinous instinct impulses and called attention only to their egoistic attributes. The aggression arising out of masculine protest became the single, all too narrow basis on which he tried to know everything living. Whether an idea was conscious or unconscious was a matter of complete indifference to him; he had almost no understanding at all of repression, and infantile sexuality did not interest him.

For Freud there could be no compromise with such a crime against the diversity of life which takes as its point of departure the prejudice of system thinking and forces it on reality instead of meticulously trying to do reality ever-greater justice through observation. For Freud this meant an unscientific simplification of the world, which he attributed to Adler's socialist ideological prejudice. Above all, Freud took offense at Adler's attempt to create a universal system without love; as he expressed it to Pfister, "He forgets the word of the apostle Paul: 'and if you have not love.'" With grim humor Freud added, "I am on the verge of visiting on him the revenge of the insulted goddess Libido."

Naturally, even Adler saw some things correctly, and in later theory formation Freud had to make concessions to him throughout. What disturbed Freud so acutely, however, was Adler's pathway to knowledge, his attempt, as it were, to assault reality with a preconceived main idea. Freud himself was accustomed to proceeding quite differently, and it seems sensible, precisely against the background of his polemical disagreement with Adler, to call to mind the various steps in the formation of the instinct theory.

Freud's psychoanalysis stands or falls with the concept of intrapsychic conflict. Only a conflict event can explain the dramatic forms of neurotic phenomena. For Freud's purposes, therefore, a monistic system that attempts to reduce everything to one common denominator is unfeasible from the beginning. For him, reality exists only in the living tension between two poles. After Freud discovered the strength and importance of sexuality, this discovery did not become a significant advance in psychoanalytic research until it became clear to him that customarily the sexual instinct was not at all well regarded and accepted by society. The fact that both his patients and his scientific public acknowledged the existence of sexual instincts with continued reluctance confirmed him in seeing here the actual battle line: on the one side the sex instincts that belong to the pleasure principle, on the other side the ego instincts that are governed by the tendency toward self-preservation. The two lie in conflict, and the deeper in the unconscious this psychic antagonism is held, the more spiritual energy it consumes. The goal of psychoanalytic therapy is to transform it into a conscious discussion. Freud believed that with this antithesis he had in felicitous fashion reproduced the folk wisdom and words of the poet according to which hunger and love rule the world. But in the long run this antithesis could not be maintained in this way.

If one wants to grant to sexuality the kind of central role in human life apparently envisioned by Freud, then one must, of course, expand and extend the concept by several nuances of meaning. The first step consisted in the very simple reflection that in itself pure sexuality, sensual love, has absolutely no inclination directed toward the long term but rather is out to "expire in satisfaction." Therefore, if it is going to become a carrier of life itself, focused on the long term, it must be provided from the beginning with purely loving—that is, in Freud's technical language, "goal-restricted"—components or experience such a conversion. Thus the sex drive is transformed step by step into eros, that force which pushes the parts of the living substance toward each other and holds them together, the inclination of all living beings of the same kind "to unite in ever more comprehensive units."

Now, when Freud investigated the ego and its special limitations more closely, however, he made the discovery that threatened with one stroke to wipe out his whole elegant polar tension, for the ego turned out to be the actual and original reservoir of the libido. It was not just that the ego henceforth had to be counted among the sex objects, and the possibility of a "narcissistic libido" had to be considered likely; research on early childhood proved unambiguously that this was something like a very elementary state of life, which in any case is there earlier than the possibility of possessing objects libidinously. With this, the antithesis between ego instincts and sex instincts was dissolved. The real threat was the danger of a kind of "pansexualism," and a large group of psychoanalysts went in that direction.

At this decisive point, Freud for better or for worse had to remember either the departed Adler or else Wilhelm Stekel, who had already to Freud's horror expressed the opinion that hate, and not love, was the primary emotional relationship between human beings. Freud was thus finally led, as he said, "to distinguish two kinds of instincts, those that are supposed to lead life to death, and the others, the sexual instincts, which repeatedly strive toward and carry out the renewal of life." Along with that, however, the nature of instincts changed in a fundamental way. If one could earlier imagine them as dynamic, forward-pressing energies, now their conservative character became clear. The actual goal of all life is death; the life instinct only delays this last instinctive goal in a kind of hesitation rhythm. Si vis vitam, para mortem—this became

Freud's motto in the last part of his life. Ultimate meaning now lay only in the gigantic contest between the two powers of death and life, in the gods Lucifer and Amor, or—as the divine pair Logos and Ananke were called in his later years—Eros and Ananke. Instincts were now, to be sure, no longer physical energies but rather resembled more "mythical beings, magnificent in their indefiniteness." Instinct theory became, so to speak, the mythology of psychoanalysis. The monistic danger seemed banished. Instincts, which from the beginning were seen in a polar tension, were still given a dual interpretation, except that the antithesis was no longer affirmed between the ego and the sex instincts but was now affirmed rather between the life instinct and the death instinct.[9]

This point of view, to be sure, very quickly involved Freud in a war on two fronts. For his concepts there lurked once again, behind an all too strong devotion to the mythical point of view, the danger of dissolving the living tension into a monistic system that Jung seemed to be bringing to psychoanalysis.

JUNG AND THE UNCONSCIOUS

In order to understand what it meant to Freud to have the Zurich psychiatrist Carl Gustav Jung (1876–1961) turn to psychoanalysis, we must first place ourselves once again in Freud's situation. Two profound personal and scientific friendships had ended in disappointment; behind him lay years of loneliness and deathly silence on the part of the scientific world. In Vienna a small group gathered only hesitantly, already weakened and decimated by the departure of Adler and his friends, and did not seem overly impressive to Freud, for in 1910, at any rate, he affirmed sarcastically that precious little of the ennobling influence of psychoanalysis was to be felt in its adherents. And now suddenly came the news that one of the most highly regarded psychiatric institutions, the "Burghölzli" clinic in Zurich, was beginning to take an interest in psychoanalysis. So with true enthusiasm Freud tried to overcome the differences that existed from the beginning. Jung, however, represented a totally foreign world for Freud, a world he was probably never able to understand fully: Jung was not a Jew but a pastor's son, and in his external appearance he towered over Freud by almost a head. He considered himself of the "hysterical" type: Freud believed he had to claim for himself the "compulsive" type. From the beginning, Jung had shown different interests from those of the Viennese physician, which all came from "exact natural science." At that time, Jung had apparently also demonstrated scientific success and was working in the middle of a recognized scientific center of psychiatry.

With single-minded energy Freud attempted right away "to build up" Jung as his successor: "I want him to acquire the authority that will warrant his later leadership of the whole movement." When this effort met with the considerable resistance of the Vienna group, he tried to bring all his personal influence to bear in order to still the waves and admonish conciliation. One would almost think that Freud supplied Jung with traits like those that would later be borne by his Egyptian Moses, that nobleman who adopted the lost Jewish remnant and led it into freedom. He publicly called Jung his Joshua, who would bring the "movement" finally into the promised land that he, Freud, had only been permitted to see from afar. Therefore, the others should develop a little masochism with regard to Jung, for "if we want to join in as Jews," we must be ready "to let some injustice be done to us."

Now, all of these hopes were to remain unfulfilled. It will probably not be possible to trace correctly what in particular led to the final break in 1914, until the correspondence between the two is available.[10] We are also not interested in the personal aspects of this human drama. For Freud's intellectual development it can only be of decisive significance to convey the intellectual challenge that Jung meant for him and how he reacted to it. In his eyes, Jung had attempted to reinterpret psychoanalytical facts "into the *abstract*, the *impersonal*, and the *ahistorical*." What did these three key words mean?

1. If Freud had to separate himself from Adler because he oriented human reality too one-sidedly toward the ego instinct, Freud now had to fear from Jung the other extreme of having psychoanalysis swamped by a monistically conceived libido theory. Freud believed he also saw system thinking in Jung, that is, a preconceived main idea that did not come from clinical observation and practice but rather was chosen "in regard to peripheral considerations." Thus it is the same reproach as that against Adler: Jung had

first created a theoretical conception of sexuality and was now seeking to capture the reality of life with it. But since this abstract concept was also conceived "mysteriously and incomprehensibly for the wise and the foolish alike" and thus no longer asserted anything concrete, the whole of psychoanalysis fell into the whirlpool of this abstraction and theorization, and in Jung's hands it lost all empirical foundation. Jung's first major paper before one of the international congresses was thus received by the circle of psychoanalysts with consternation, because it was believed that the etiological dynamics of the pathological event were neglected in favor of a monistic interpretation.

2. Freud ascribed a considerable part of the therapeutic effect of psychoanalysis to the fact that in analysis the patients learned some very personal things. By being confronted very concretely with embarrassing and painful feelings and memories, they learned to deal with them and to solve the related problems differently and better than they had during childhood. In Freud's eyes, however, Jung depersonalized these experiences at that moment in which he no longer tried to understand concretely but sought to understand only symbolically the problems that were related, for example, to the Oedipus situation—so that, for example, it was not at all the mother who was desired but only the "unreachable," and the conflict was supposed to be carried out no longer with the father but only with an "intellectual principle." Yet most bitter for Freud was the impression he received that Jung, like Breuer, was stumbling over the offensiveness of sexual matters, since he apparently thought that even if one must recognize the truth of certain things, they may not be proclaimed in public, because one would undermine civilization and block the impulse toward sublimation. When Jung even urged his students not to speak with patients about "unclean" things in any detail because it would be too unpleasant when meeting them again later in society, Freud's judgment was certain: for Jung as well as for Breuer it was still a question of suppressing the sexual element. Once again the "primitive, powerful melody of instinct" was not heard, and the personal element was thereby forfeited; only a few cultural overtones were picked out,[11] and therapy sank to the level of poor pastoral care: instead of liberating analytically, every hour brought only new demands,

such as those for inner concentration through introversion, for religious intensification, or for a radical transformation of the whole inner self.[12] But where is one supposed to get the strength for that?

3. Finally, when Freud felt that the shift that took place through Jung was in the direction of the ahistorical, he obviously meant by this that Jung's research into symbols led to his regarding the unconscious not as a stage to be passed through and overcome but as a source of profound wisdom that one must maintain and cultivate. Freud feared that Jung had turned to folk myths and the study of heretics not in order to see this material in its historical relativity and perhaps draw on it as an aid to understanding but in order to honor in it a high ideal to which one must return. By seeing the actual source of wisdom in the unconscious as the nonrational, Jung, in Freud's opinion, came precariously close to a position in which psychology is presented as a new gospel of salvation or a new ideology. Freud objected to the "regressive direction" in anything that ran the risk of turning human reality into ahistorical metaphysics and thereby misunderstanding it.

Thus parted the two ways. Freud continued working consciously in a direction that singled out everything that reflected Aryan religion, in order neatly to cut it off. This did not happen without animosities here and there, and they went so deep that cooperation became forever impossible, even where later theoretical developments occasionally showed converging tendencies. Full of bitter hate, Freud called after the Joshua he had previously honored so highly, that his bad theories did not compensate for his unpleasant character. "So, then, we are finally rid of them, the brutal Saint Jung and those who parrot him!" Jung, on the other hand, revenged himself through the unfortunate idea of speaking of a "Jewish psychology" that one may not apply to Christian Teutons.

The Jung episode made it necessary for Freud to subject his theory of the unconscious to ever new examinations. We would like briefly to state the most important results.

Before Freud the view was generally held—with few exceptions, such as that of Theodor Lipps—that the object of psychology was human consciousness, and the impossibility of an unconscious psychic state was logically proved from the definition of the psychic. Everything spiritual that became active and intensive could also become conscious, and the only pathway to knowledge was, and largely still is today, self-observation and experimentation, the results of which are objectified into psychological knowledge. According to this view, a latent and therefore unconscious idea can never become the object of psychology. All phenomena that lie beyond the realm of human consciousness must consequently be rejected or judged as meaningless phenomena peripheral to the psychic.

From the beginning of his psychological research, Freud made the attempt to penetrate precisely this mysterious area that transcended consciousness. The unconscious was for him the "actual psychic reality," just as unknown, to be sure, as reality in the outside world. He believed the correction that Kant had undertaken in our conception of the outer world had to be expanded into the realm of the psychic, and he attempted tirelessly to show that there are psychic processes "that are actively at work and yet do not reach consciousness." The fact that everything substantial and new in human intellectual activity comes from sudden ideas whose provenience we do not know, and the experience that we have access to the results of thought processes whose origins remain unknown—these necessitate finally the assumption that every psychic act begins unconsciously and that in the unconscious we rediscover "the undisciplined and indestructible in the human soul," the actually demonic.

In this Freud set himself in opposition to the reigning, and in his time undisputed, scientific conviction that the character of reality was to be conferred only on what was objectifiable through immediate experience. In its place Freud put the staunchly held postulate of the unity of meaning of all psychic processes and believed that with the striving for meaning and relationship he had found a fully warranted scientific motif that could also transcend immediate experience. If psychology had previously gained its basic finding that a human being has consciousness through an analogical connection between personal experience and knowledge of the "alien soul," then Freud thought that psychoanalysis was justified in demanding "that this connecting procedure also be turned toward one's own person," and that "all of the acts and utterances that I note in myself and do not know how to relate to the rest of my psychic life" be judged "as if they belonged to another person."

Thus Freud demanded the recognition of realms that are not objectifiable; indeed, inherent in objectification is a concept of object that distinguishes observing subject and observed object from each other in the making of a judgment. This is not possible in regard to the phenomena of the unconscious; they can become conscious only with self-dissolution. Hence Freud ventured for the first time a discussion of phenomena "whose nature included the fact that they could not be described in the form of complete objectification." This would later find its justification through quantum physics, for even with the electron, observation requires modifying intrusions; and in both areas it is a question of facts and regularities "that in logical structure correspond exactly to the concept of complementarity." Objectifying knowledge is replaced by meaningful understanding.

For Freud the perception that one can know something from the unconscious only after it has experienced a transfer into consciousness meant methodologically first of all the use of inference from conscious effect back to unconscious psychic process. One cannot observe unconscious processes themselves, but one can seek to understand them on the basis of other indications and evidence. This indirect evidence, however, is almost equivalent to the direct evidence offered by consciousness, for it offers the possibility of seeing very clearly the characteristic traits of the unconscious. It has been shown, that is, that in the unconscious, validity is given to a conceptual structure that has become alien to our conscious minds but clearly governs the formation of dreams, the free association of ideas, and errors such as slips of the tongue. We also find it in the myths, fairy tales, sagas, sayings, and jokes of the folk tradition. This conceptual structure is distinguished by the fact that in it the laws of logical thinking, especially the principle of contradiction, are not valid and there is no connection with time or numbers.[13] Freud studied this characteristic of the unconscious in its offspring, which he designated "hybrids" and which appeared primarily as fantasies but also were expressed in neurotic symptoms and above all in dreams. Here it was especially the characteristic phenomenon of symbol formation that stimulated Freud to reflect.

The great discovery that Freud made with his hysteria patients was that language can become a surrogate for action, and on this he based the possibilities of his therapy. Language, however, then had to have a far greater significance than that of a conventional agreement on a certain, fixed character of portrayal: it had to possess, rather, the capability of representation, of substitution. Freud saw this capability concentrated in the possibility of symbol formation. Indeed, he repeatedly observed a "symbolic relationship between the cause and the psychological phenomena" of the symptoms of hysteria patients. They are the "mnemonic symbol of certain effective [traumatic] impressions and experiences." Thus in neurosis as well as psychosis there can be a full-scale "reality substitution" by a symbol. For the patient, the symbol replaces a piece of lost reality and represents it in such a way that he actually participates in it.

Yet this representative function of the symbol is in no way limited to the realm of psychopathology. In dreams every healthy person participates in the formation of a representational symbolism that is not at all characteristic of the dreamer alone; it binds him also to the unconscious ideas of the myths, sagas, expressions, proverbs, and jokes of the tradition in which he stands. As psychoanalysis spread into other language areas, it became evident that the commonality of symbolism extends even beyond the commonality of language and apparently penetrates and binds the whole of humanity. In striving to explain the genesis of this highly characteristic state of affairs, Freud assumed that "what today is bound symbolically was probably united through conceptual and linguistic identity in primitive times," and that there must have been an old, now extinct mode of expression, a kind of rudimentary language, of which symbolic relationships are the remnants. Yet the most astonishing thing about this phenomenon is that it develops independent of tradition and teaching and is encountered even in very small children. Freud decided therefore on the assumption that symbols must be a piece of "ancient spiritual inheritance" that "has no other source than inherited transference," so that one must speak of "innate symbolism."

This postulates nothing less than a participation in tradition that is not conveyed through historical testimonies. That, if it should prove to be justified, places the hermeneutical problem in a new context. Freud could thus define more precisely what, as the "foundation of human nature in general," had played so great a role in the history of hermeneutics and what was previously circumscribed inexactly and vaguely with the catchwords "life" and "understanding of existence":

> The content of the unconscious in general is indeed the collective, common possession of humanity. We will, for the moment, resort to the use of analogies. The processes that we are studying here in the lives of peoples are very similar to those known to us from psychopathology, and yet not entirely the same ones. We have finally reached the conclusion that the psychic consequences of those primitive times became an inheritance and in every new generation need only to be awakened, not acquired. We think at this point of the example of the assuredly "innate" symbolism that originated in the time of the development of language, is familiar to every child without receiving any instruction, and is the same with all peoples in spite of language differences. What we may still lack in certainty we can get from other results of psychoanalytic research. We learn that our children react in a number of significant respects not as befits their own experience but according to instinct, comparable to animals, in a way that is only explainable through phylogenetic acquisition.

For Freud, hints of the unconscious did not evoke helplessness and sorrow; he tried to follow them and clear a path into these areas through interpretation. Indeed, the relevance of the material that was presented to him by patients in the form of memories, ideas, and dreams was not revealed until the material was interpreted. That means that it had to be related to a context of meaning that was not even known to the patient. He had to press forward from the patient's ideas to what was repressed, from the distortions of dreams to the distortion itself. This was a job that Freud could only compare with the labor of the gold miner. Out of the ore of ideas and dreams, the precious metal of repressed thoughts had to be recovered. Psychoanalysis had to develop itself first of all into an "art of interpretation." Instructions had to be given for "how one is to understand." Freud modestly described them as a series of "empirically acquired rules," of which the one to be regarded as the most important and most amazing is that the analyst must "with evenhanded attention turn himself over to his own unconscious intellectual activity," in order to detect the patient's unconscious with his own unconscious.

It is indeed one of the most notable observations of psychoanalysis "that the unconscious of a person can react to the unconscious of another while bypassing consciousness."

This, to be sure, did not in any way mean some kind of irrational or mystical practice but simply meant doing justice to the hermeneutical circle that governs all processes of understanding. The analyst had to be asked "by his own means" to achieve a translation of unconscious materials. The goal was to obtain a satisfactory meaning by setting the material "tentatively" into another context of meaning and laying before the patient this interpretation for renewed associative confirmation or disagreement. It had to rest on the analyst's thorough knowledge of symbols.

At this point, however, came the greatest difficulties. Symbols are always ambiguous and equivocal. They stand for representative substitutions on the basis of similarities, but the point of comparison escapes our knowledge. "One senses a conditionality but does not know wherein it consists." Even to the end of his life Freud himself was prevented from determining more closely the foundation and conditionality of symbols, but he could at least provide the direction in which further research had to be done: it consisted in the effort to move from the symbolism that lay behind myths to an interpretation of dreams and vice versa. This stimulus had a productive influence on the research efforts of a whole generation and only in recent times has come to a standstill.

Freud proved, however, to be more fortunate in regard to the other rules of interpretation that he gave and developed as examples. Even if one was not able to press forward in dreams to a clear perception of supraindividual participation in symbol formation, one could still work out the individual contribution that every dreamer made to the distortion of his dream. Freud called this "dreamwork" and recognized that in addition to symbol formation, it consisted of condensation and displacement processes whose mechanism could be investigated precisely in the so-called primary process. In this case the interpretation consists in taking up the dreamwork. This occurs through linguistic means, the function of which is to see "that even internal processes in the ego acquire the quality of consciousness"; indeed, in the conscious concept the objective concept is united with the word concept, whereas in the unconscious the objective concept is alone.

Since the dreamwork brings the latent dream idea into contact with an "archaic system of expression," as it were, it lets thoughts experience a regressive treatment. This direction can only become progressive if the repressed is "recognized as past, devalued, and deprived of its investment of emotional energy." This can happen, however, only if the unconscious concepts "have become conscious through analytical work" and "a part of one's forgotten prior history" is placed before the analyst.

Even if Freud resisted imagining "that the unconscious is something put aside, a rudimentary organ, a residue of development,"[14] in the act of its becoming conscious he had doubtless still seen a "further development" and a "forward step." A lack of consciousness meant a step backward and captivity to the past; consciousness and interpretation meant freedom for the future: "What was id, shall become ego," for psychoanalysis is a tool "that is supposed to enable the ego progressively to conquer the id."

4

THE THERAPY

Healing through Language

Thus far Freud's theories had developed out of interaction with his
scientific opponents. The question remained open as to what contribution practical therapy made to theory formation. To this day
there is disagreement among Freud's interpreters over whether one
should attach the greater significance to his practice or to his formation of theory. The crux of the theological polemic was repeatedly found in the attempt to free Freud from his ideological
background and make his practical methods productive for pastoral care.[1] In similar fashion philosophers and sociologists tried to
make a fundamental distinction between the concreteness of psychoanalytical practice on the one hand and, on the other, the abstractions of the theories, which could also be applied to other
areas of life. This can lead either to the view—held by Arnold
Gehlen and Karl Stern—that psychoanalysis is useful only in
the realm of individual therapy[2] and that any introduction into the
areas beyond psychology is "unwarranted," or to the view of Herbert Marcuse and Norman Brown, for example, that Freud's psychology of the individual is really, "according to its actual essence,
social psychology" and must be reshaped into a "broad, general .
theory of human nature, culture, and history," which in turn must
raise the consciousness of humanity as a whole to a new level,
that is, must "almost immediately" become social criticism.

Thus the forced separation of theory and practice in the interpretation of Freud runs the risk of emphasizing one side too strongly

and neglecting the other. We will not be able to do justice to Freud unless we inquire about the contributions of both sides and bring them into relationship with each other. Not only Freud's theories but also his practice contained revolutionary tendencies. They will be developed in what follows by looking at the role that Freud accorded to language in his therapy, because it is precisely here that the view of the individual and of interpersonal relationships was fundamentally transformed. In order to make this role even clearer, it will be related to linguistic reflections that have also appeared in modern theology. Perhaps in that way one important point can be made: Freud's work can be understood as a challenge to the Christian faith not just on the basis of the specific writings of religious criticism in his later years, which are subject to ideological suspicion, but at the heart of his whole psychoanalytical work, namely, in the pathways he discovered in therapy.

EXCURSUS: LANGUAGE AND THEOLOGICAL HERMENEUTICS

Apparently, at the beginning of human intellectual activity—as far as we are able to survey it—stands the belief in language as a foreordained fact of life, intrinsic to human existence as such. By participating in it, a person participates in the essence that reveals and conveys itself to him in language. The "archaic" definition of the human soul consists precisely in the fact that it is the organ of language, and the old Chaldean translations of Gen. 2:7 render this passage very profoundly when they say that through the breath of God man becomes a רוּחַ מְמַלְלָה, a speaking spirit. In the ancient Greek world the primitive function of language was designated with the stem μυ, which is among those primal words that still have a contrary sense and that can designate remaining silent as well as speaking; and this is the mark of the true, living word and authentic speech. According to Plato this linguistic disclosure was handed down by the "ancients," who, however, added nothing of their own but simply passed on what they had received. Since it draws nothing from the self but comes ἐξ ἀκοῆσ—from a hearing event—it has the power to save when one believes it.

In contrast to this, a totally new principle is introduced as soon as the need emerges to achieve ambiguity in language as opposed to demonstrable, objectifiable singleness of meaning. This seems to have been the case for the first time in the Pythagorean tradition, in which the number was ranked above language and given highest praise by thinkers such as Philolaos: without numbers, according to him, it is impossible to consider or to know anything. The nature of the number dispenses knowledge and provides guidance and instruction for everyone. Its nature can never accept lies, for truth is characteristic and innate in the family of numbers. Thus a new logos is formed that is derived from a principle other than linguistic thinking, namely, from the regularity of numbers. The numerical way of thinking was taken over into psychology by Aristotle, who could even say, "The soul itself is a moving number." For him thinking was equivalent to the sum of one's thoughts, which come uniformly one after another like numbers. His work that later became known under the title "Hermeneutics" is nothing more than a discussion of the principle of contradiction. Since he had thus developed language on the level of concept and with its formal structure of deductions and derivations brought about a logical analysis on the basis of the subject-object model, a new kind of existence through arithmetic and geometry could be created. It rested completely on the compulsion toward contradiction-free thinking, which can recognize as reality only "what can be described as a form of universally valid law." Thus arises a conception of language in which it is regarded more or less exclusively as an instrument for the transmission of thoughts and knowledge, and that means, ultimately, information. On this foundation were built concepts that had language consist (as in Herder's view) of "completely unessential noises, sounds, and ciphers, which have only the value of counters," or that (as in the mathematical conceptual structure of Descartes) can admit as truth only what can be represented as a "certainty equivalent to arithmetical and geometrical proofs."

In his early works Wittgenstein made an attempt to transform language into pure information, that is, to reduce linguistic understanding to knowing "what is the case." But he had either to declare that most of the statements and questions of philosophy were nonsense or to give up the effort itself as impossible. Science's conception of language is apparently still at this point today.

Suddenly we recall Wilhelm von Humboldt, who as early as

almost one hundred years ago called attention to the impossibility of transforming language completely into information because in it something unknown is always left over. Every word adds to a concept "significantly from itself," and since no one thinks with the same word exactly the same thing as another, even the smallest difference sends vibrations through the whole language, and all understanding is at the same time always a misunderstanding.

Werner Heisenberg (*Physics and Philosophy*) has shown that even in the realm of modern physics one can no longer make objectifying statements that assert that their content does not depend on the conditions under which they can be verified. We cannot even describe the world without speaking of ourselves, and the concept of "probability function," formulated by Heisenberg, gives eloquent expression to this connection between objective and subjective elements. Thus even for the later Wittgenstein the real nature of language became something that lies inside, beneath the surface, and is only to be dug out through an analysis. He discovered thereby the dimension of depth, for which something like a "deep grammar" must be created; and if these efforts come very close to being a therapy, then the philosopher must treat a question as an illness.

Above all, however, it was Heidegger who passed judgment on modern metaphysical thinking, which turns everything that is into a "calculatingly controllable and transparent object" and accomplishes its objectification in a "placing before" that aims at "bringing before oneself everything that is, so that the calculating person can be sure—and that means certain—of what is." Heidegger placed such thinking under the verdict of "forgetfulness of being," *Seinsvergessenheit*, which also applies to axiology, in which he was also able to discover a most intimate relationship to a "so much," to a quantity and number. Especially the later Heidegger regarded reason, which had been exalted for centuries, as the most persistent adversary of thinking. True to his principle that history is the "recurrence of the possible," for whose decisive repetition existence is supposed to hold itself open "fatefully at every moment," he attempted a recourse to linguistic and conceptual structures that precede the logicalization of language and the mathematicization of being: namely, the true logos and its essence, which appeared in the beginnings of thought. He made thinking dependent on the communication of being and turned to the poet as the actual priest of humanity through whom "the language speaks." It is the business of thinking "to bring to expression ever and again the continuing arrival of being, waiting in its continuing on humanity," and to gather language into a simple speaking, for language is the "house of being." Thus may the understanding of language be forced back into the oraclelike origin of the conceptual structure of myth.

Thus arises the question, How can a theology that has set as a goal for itself the overcoming of this mythical thought structure accomplish this task without subjecting itself to the danger described above and still do justice to the fundamental human essence as language? Rudolf Bultmann saw the philosophy of Heidegger as especially suited to working out a "proper exposition of human existence," not least of all because he shared the latter's aversion to any anthropology in which he could see only an interpretation of humanity "that basically knows already what a human being is and therefore can never ask who he is." Heidegger expressly warned against any psychology as the "relentless dismemberment of the inner life by curiosity-seekers" and as "analytical staring at spiritual conditions and their backgrounds"; the relationship of these conditions to the existence of others is regarded by him as only a "projection of one's own being within oneself into the being of another."[3] Therefore he imposed upon himself so great a restraint in regard to human existence that he limited himself to comprehending its structures and clarifying their existential formality. For Bultmann, however, it was precisely this bracketing of the human realm that made this conceptual system appear so well suited and appropriate for theological hermeneutics. For "God's transcendence and the transcendence of my actual self belong together. . . . With this transcendent God a person has communion only in openness to the unavailable future. . . . This readiness, however, . . . is nothing other than the readiness for my transcendent self standing before me." Now, the task of proclamation must be to make the implicit understanding of existence explicit and, through this making conscious, to ensure that existence can come more and more into its own and that its behavior toward the things that matter remains a "moving, living relationship."

This process was now developed by Bultmann (*Jesus Christ and*

Mythology) into the "hermeneutical principle," according to which "appropriate conceptions" must be discovered that will keep in operation the correct questions regarding the possibilities of human existence. Indeed, understanding can come only from a particular formulation of the question, from a direction in the questioning. Thus, this progressing, living relationship to the matter guides the direction of the questioning out of which the particular hermeneutical principle grows. Bultmann delegated to philosophy, as its task, this absolutely fundamental working-out of any theological hermeneutic, because it was in any case an illusion that the exposition could be independent of worldly conceptions. Bultmann then expressed his deep conviction that the conceptual scheme of philosophy was adequate only if it grew "out of the understanding of human existence as a temporal-historical one." The most appropriate conceptions for understanding human existence were thus offered by that philosophical school in which human existence is the direct object of consideration and human essence is described as historical essence, and therefore my existence lies within my personal responsibility. Such is the case with existential philosophy. With the challenge "You must exist!"—that is, take responsibility for yourself—it makes one open to the Word of the Bible, open for decision, open to the future.

Here lies Bultmann's real interest. If God is to be understood as the "transcendent in the midst of the transitory," as the "unconditioned in the conditioned," as the "eternal at any given time in the present" whose futurity is his transcendence, then this is possible only in an understanding that is at the same time also a decision, which Bultmann called historical understanding. Just as historical knowledge is never completed because to a historical event belongs its future, so to historical understanding belongs its character of decision, its openness to the future, and thereby it recognizes the "nonderivability of the moment." The decision that is required here can be reduced to the formula of whether a person intends to understand being out of the reality of what is at hand or out of the reality of the moment. With this understanding of a human being as a historical being in the true sense, Bultmann believed that he was ensured against the idea that belief was only a subjective psychological event. With this historical understanding he also saw the

subject and object schema annulled, and he believed that the desired "nonobjectifying way of thinking and speaking had been
found."

This way was concentrated in the realms of personal being that
do not open themselves to objectifying eyes and are only experienced in the existential encounter as love, trust, goodness, and so
forth. These human accomplishments and relationships do not
proceed, according to Bultmann, as a natural process but are
constantly open to questions and can only be won or lost in my
decisions, which are not derivable from anything previous. As
existential exegesis, they do not like to be the object of observation, for I cannot examine my own decisions; they are always
ventures in the personal relationship of trust and of love. At this
decisive point, where Bultmann intended by process of analogy to
understand the grace of God, stands the word "mystery." Friendship, love, and loyalty are, that is, mysteries in the same way as the
grace of God.

At this point we would like to set forth the questions whose
answers will move our discussion forward, answers that we hope
to find in Freud:

1. Bultmann permitted as key concepts only such fulfillments of
personal being that, in his opinion, elude objective thinking and
therefore must finally be addressed as mysteries because they do
not hold still for objective viewing. Yet, we would like to ask, is not
the critical thinking with which Bultmann himself warned against a
"not seldom illegitimate recourse to mystery"—is it not suspended
here a little prematurely? Does not the thought of miracles—which
indeed, according to Bultmann, has become unfeasible and ought to
be abandoned—does it not thereby persist in regard to personal life?
Are love, friendship, loyalty, duty, and conscience actually categories of mystery that must remain closed to science? Is there not
thus created a holy area of taboos no longer to be questioned, which
in their irrationality represent the arsenal of Bultmann's existential
interpretation? And as for the "existential character" of our experiences, which Bultmann would like to have made absolutely assured,
is it not a euphemistic expression for the condition of the uncon-
sciousness of mythical thinking, which Heidegger in a magnificent

curve guides us back to? With his irreverent questions, Freud also extended to human existence the process of making conscious, which has now become our destiny; should we not be able to follow him easier there than Heidegger in his return to myth?

2. Bultmann took for granted that there is a difference in essence and in principle between the knowledge of natural and of historical phenomena: natural phenomena permit objective thinking whereas historical phenomena elude it. Since myth is seen from the standpoint of "primitive science," it shares objective thinking with modern science, whose instrument is considered to be language. Thus Bultmann had to resort to a twofold concept of reality, for the thinking of natural science cannot comprehend the total reality of the world and of human life. In faith I learn that this present world is not the only world.

Now, it would be mistaken, however, to characterize mythical thinking as objective thinking; that still lies completely outside its possibilities. Only a literal, word-for-word understanding objectifies. Even when one ascribes to language merely an objectifying function, that may at the very least be termed one-sided. Moreover, Bultmann operated with an outdated conception of natural science. We have already seen that today even the language of the natural scientist can no longer be purely objective. Of course, Bultmann's conviction that the distinction between subject and object was to be completely excluded from the question of human existence must doubtless be termed an illusion: the hermeneutical circle of the speech event is completed only in the proper joining of the two possibilities. Without doubt Freud went from the intellectual presuppositions of a purely objectifying science to the analysis of human existence. Yet by recognizing language as its most important possibility, his thinking changed in a way that might also be of interest to theology.

3. Thus Bultmann's hermeneutic apparently suffered from insufficient contact with the progressive tendencies of the other sciences. We would like to extend this also to the question of the basic feeling for life of people in our day. Certainly a look at modern literature as a source of knowledge about humankind may be helpful, but is it not too narrow a basis for this important area of all

linguistic expository work? If the experience of the "nonderivability of the moment" is made the center of decisive life experience, which is supposed to provide access to faith, that obviously presupposes that the people of our day exist with the basic feeling of this freedom. Freud believed that in accordance with his experience he had to assert the opposite, and he repeatedly pointed to how little a person is "master in his own house" and how necessary it is first to liberate him for this freedom. When one, therefore, attempts to make freedom the hermeneutical principle of humanity, one has taken as the starting point what can only be considered the goal of the hermeneutical operation. Let no one object that the understanding of humanity developed by Freudian psychoanalysis concerns only a small pathological minority. There is, to be sure, a quantitative but not a fundamental, qualitative difference between the neurotic and the so-called normal spiritual life; and Freudian analyses have apparently proved to be more effective than those of Heidegger.[4]

4. We must call attention to one more point. Bultmann demonstrated that even Christian proclamation does not lie outside the hermeneutical circle of the processes of linguistic understanding. It is not, therefore, primarily an announcement of a new knowledge but the uncovering of a knowledge that I have already, which includes the process of anamnesis and lifts the prior understanding into consciousness. This suggests the dynamic of the historical in the process of the speech event. It may be striking that Freud could describe the therapeutic process with almost the same words. For him too, it was a matter of a removal of the amnesia, of a recalling to mind that liberates from the compulsion to repeat and opens the pathway to the future.

In a time when the synoptic view of the various areas of life again lies somewhat nearer than in the immediate past, it may not be very astonishing to discover surprising parallels between theological and nontheological conceptual structures. This brings to bear, vis-à-vis theological hubris, the veritable "compulsion to think" of the historical moment. Yet such a parallelism will not be fruitful theologically until it is raised to the methodological clarity of a dialogue within which the two partners listen to each other and want to learn from each other. With this intention, we now turn again to Freud and his discussion of language within psychoanalysis.

LANGUAGE AS MEANS OF THERAPY

Freud's first, tentative efforts to introduce language into the healing arts as a means of therapy actually occurred in glaring contradiction to what we described above as the nature of language in the circular structure of the dialogue. For Freud, educated in the medical tradition of his time, the patient was at first nothing more than the "object" of diagnostic research and therapeutic influence. What he learned with Jean-Martin Charcot and Hippolyte Bernheim was simply that the "instruments" suitable for this influence were not only the scalpel and medicines but also language. Thus it was completely in this instrumental sense that he first viewed and employed language. When it happened that the symptoms of the patient could not be objectified as caused by a particular organ but apparently came from a "counter-will" in the person himself, this counter-will had to be attacked head-on through the therapeutic will of the doctor. The only question was how one might achieve for the doctor the kind of authority that could prove stronger and superior to the pathogenic counter-will of the patient. Charcot and Bernheim found a way to do this with hypnosis, that is, with a particular technique that made it possible through artifice to set aside the patient's conscious self-control to the extent that he fell into a sleeplike, somnambulant condition; this made it possible to bypass consciousness and place the suggestive commands of the doctor directly inside the patient.

Freud applied this method successfully for the first time with a woman who, after giving birth, had fallen into an acute condition of depression because of an anxious expectation that she would not be able to suckle her child. The suggestion that was made under hypnosis, "Have no fear: you will nurse quite well," resolved the difficulty with a single stroke. A year later, of course, when the next child was born, it was a question of overcoming the same calamity again; the method proved to have its value simply in alleviating symptoms but not in healing causes. The counter-will within the patient had merely been replaced by the authority of the doctor, which held sway only as long as its effectiveness was repeatedly renewed by suggestion.

As he attempted a scientific explanation of the phenomena in these hysterical illnesses, which consisted in the hysterical person's being overcome by an affect whose cause he claimed to know nothing about, Freud determined that the traditional conceptual models of medicine actually had nothing helpful to offer. Thus he resolutely left the pathways of thought marked out by Charcot and turned to a conceptual world that, for a scientist in the closing years of the nineteenth century, must be regarded as extremely odd. He believed in all seriousness that the medieval interpretation of hysterical phenomena as possession by a demon came closer to the truth than the medical theories of his time and that it must merely be demythologized.[5]

The result of such a conceptual procedure is simple. The hysterical person finds himself in a spiritual condition in which the uniting of all impressions and memories from the past is no longer possible; that is, these have made themselves independent, as it were. They have freed themselves from the ego and therefore, like an ego-alien "demon," cause emotions and actions that the patient can neither understand and explain nor prevent. But how can such a separation of mental processes from the ego of the conscious person come about? Freud could see the cause in nothing other than the incompatibility of an emotion with the person's conscious goals and tendencies and in the resolution of this conflict through the flat denial of the emotion. The process is thus as follows: An experience, an idea, or a feeling awakens a painful emotion because, for example, it cannot be brought into agreement with the moral concepts of the person concerned. Thus he decides to forget it because he does not believe himself capable of intellectually working through the contradiction of this idea with his ego. This forgetting, however, is not successful; it leads to a split in consciousness, and the sum of excitation thus liberated is converted into the physical and leads to hysterical symptoms.

As soon as this becomes clear, however, one can no longer hold fast to the single approach of suggestively influencing the patient. The therapeutic task now presented itself in a different way, as Josef Breuer had already seen very clearly in the development of his "cathartic method." He had long struggled with this "sum of excitation" that the hysterical person customarily transformed into physical symptoms. Another way of disposing of it had to be created. At this point the patient's use of language came into play: the disposal of the excitation could be brought about through speech, with the help of which the individual could dissipate the emotion.

This phase of the development of an effective psychotherapy through words, in which Breuer and Freud were still operating on common ground, took place completely under the influence of the physical-physiological conceptual model, in which language—far from any mutual reciprocity—was accorded only the value of a "discharge of throttled emotions through speech," just as Darwin had explained the tail wagging of a dog as the draining-off of excitement. From the doctor's standpoint it was no longer a matter of suggestively influencing the symptom itself but was a matter of an "inquiry under hypnosis" that occasionally could take the form of a "rigorous interrogation," in order to uncover the sources of the conflict and make its resolution possible. Also the "instructive influence" that Freud had occasionally practiced in therapy outside hypnosis and which had consisted of "affirmation, prohibition, and the introduction of contrary ideas of every sort" now receded more and more, because the patient could very quickly counter its effect through an act of the will. Instead of this, Freud went after the individual symptom's developmental history in order to be able to battle its presuppositions. This was the path that took him further and further from Breuer's cathartic method and allowed him to seek his own ways.

There were two experiences that made Freud proceed on this path to scientific independence. First, Freud proved to be a poor hypnotist. His suggestive abilities were subject to limits that he himself connected with his nature.[6] Therefore, once when a patient came to him whom he could not hypnotize, he abruptly gave up hypnosis, requested only "concentration," and established the supine position and the optional closing of the eyes as means for achieving this concentration. He then reached back to the proof that Bernheim had adduced years before that the memories a patient produces under hypnotic somnambulism are only *apparently* forgotten in the waking state and can be called forth again by mild admonition "connected with a grasp that is supposed to indicate another state of consciousness." Thus arose the method of "pressing"; that is, with light pressure Freud laid his hand on the patient, at the same time assuring him that in this way the memories lying behind his symptom would come to mind.

Freud's second experience occurred during a vacation. A relative of the owner of the inn in which Freud was staying secretly followed him on a walk in order to consult with him regarding her nervous ailment. He asked himself the question, Could perhaps a simple dialogue be successful? He asked the girl "to continue to say whatever occurred to her, in the sure expectation that whatever occurred to her" would be just what he needed to shed light on her case, and he discovered that it really worked. The new method took more effort but brought great progress: it achieved insight into the motives that were of prime importance for the "forgetting" of memories.

In the famous case of Elisabeth von R., Freud accomplished for the first time with the help of dialogue a layer-by-layer clearing-away of pathogenic psychic material, which he could only compare with the techniques of archaeology. In the process he learned that a pure speaking-out, a kind of "life confession," had no therapeutic value. Not until attention is called to the "resistance" that directs itself against the expression of certain things does it become apparent that behind this resistance stands the energy that once banished the unbearable affect from consciousness. Freud's therapeutic effort was now directed toward the overcoming of these resistances in the dialogue through interpretation.

Thus it came down to the formation of a method that remained unfeasible "without the full cooperation and willing attention" of the patient. Hence such a session proceeded "as a dialogue between two equally conscious persons," within which Freud sought to mobilize the intellectual interest of the patient and endeavored to get him to be a colleague, so to speak. A reciprocal partnership was thereby achieved, and henceforth one could ascertain the "greatest possible contrast" between suggestive technique and analytical therapy. With that, however, the problems were just beginning. Even if from then on the patient himself determined the theme of the daily work, the analytical relationship still had to remain asymmetrical, for in it interpretation was supposed to make conscious, and making conscious was supposed to heal. Thus it seemed unavoidable that for a period of time the personal relationship with the doctor would push itself unduly into the foreground. For this reason Breuer turned away from common research work, and Freud saw himself faced with the task of devoting his special attention to the interpersonal events between doctor and patient and, following the theme of the opposition of "transference and countertransference," with the task of discovering the "hermeneutical circle" in these phenomena too.

INTERPRETATION AS INTERPERSONAL EVENT

In researching the unconscious, Freud had already in his *Traumdeutung* (The interpretation of dreams) turned from the topical approach—which could regard the conscious and the unconscious as two regions that were spatially separable from each other, and which he valued only as a conceptual model anyway—to the dynamic approach, which worked with the concept of cathexis (*Energiebesetzung*, the investment of mental and emotional energy) and did not localize psychic structures in the organic elements of the nervous system at all "but rather, so to speak, *between* them." In the further course of his research effort, the dynamic viewpoint became more important to the extent that the work with resistance and the power game of transference and countertransference became the actual center of psychoanalysis. Freud himself described his discovery in this field:

> The origin of a certain hysterical symptom in one of my woman patients was a desire that had been entertained many years ago and immediately banished into the unconscious; it was the wish that the man with whom she was carrying on a conversation at the time would boldly seize the opportunity and force a kiss upon her. Then one time, after the close of a session, such a desire surfaced in the patient in regard to my person; she was appalled by it, passed a sleepless night, and in the next session, although she did not refuse treatment, she was totally useless for work. After I learned of the obstacle and removed it, the work went forward again; and note: the desire that frightened the patient appeared as the next one of her pathogenic memories, the one then required by logical connection. It happened this way: first, the content of the desire came into the consciousness of the patient without the memories of the attendant circumstances that could shift this desire into the past; through the compulsion to associate that dominates the conscious mind, the desire now present was

connected with my person, which was permitted to occupy the patient's mind; and with this misalliance—which I call false connection—the same affect was awakened that earlier forced the patient to banish this forbidden desire. Now that I have learned this, I can presuppose in regard to any similar claim on my person that a transference and false connection have again occurred.

If this mental mechanism is not recognized, it can maneuver not only the therapeutic but also the pedagogical and pastoral relationship into ever new impasses. With this simple as well as brilliant insight came a decisive broadening of the horizon of understanding in interpersonal dynamics. Freud's patients gradually learned to understand "that with such transferences to the person of the doctor, it is a question of a compulsion and an illusion that will subside with the termination of analysis." Freud defined transferences as "new editions, reproductions of the stimulations and fantasies that are to be awakened and made conscious during the process of analysis, with the characteristic substitution of the person of the doctor for an earlier person." One cannot avoid it through any means in any interpersonal relationship; in psychoanalytical healing, it is merely a question of resolving it, that is, of uncovering it and explaining it to the patient. If this succeeds, then what appeared at first to be the greatest hindrance to psychoanalysis can become the most powerful means of help; for the patient experiences again in his relationship to the doctor the part of his emotional life that he can no longer call back into memory, and only through such a reliving will he be convinced of the existence and power of this unconscious excitation and be able "in the increased temperature of the transference experience" to be freed of the symptoms. "In this reaction the doctor plays . . . the role of a catalytic agent."

Starting with these basic findings, Freud granted to transference the central position within his psychoanalytical technique. After that, treatment proceeded to a certain extent as a struggle between the therapist and the patient, in which the patient wants to act out his passions and feelings, that is, to rehearse and portray them, while the doctor wants to force him "to subject them to thoughtful consideration."

But just where is this master plate made that is, "in the course of life, regularly duplicated and printed anew"? On the basis of his clinical material, Freud could only infer that the patient's need for love is not completely satisfied by reality, so that he must "turn to every new person with libidinous ideas and expectations." The doctor is also set into one of these "psychic series" that thus arise, whose constellation, however, can be shaped already by the mental images of father, mother, brother, and sister. Thus, which transference the patient makes depends on the "peculiarity acquired during childhood years, which love conditions he sets, which instincts he satisfies, which goals he sets." Hence transference is a matter of duplicating "infantile imagoes,"[7] the dramatic high point of which—as is well known—Freud considered to be the Oedipus complex, which for him became the actual point of origin of transferences. The neutral person of the doctor becomes the deputy and surrogate of the father or brother; the instinctual forces have retreated into regression; they have turned from reality and falsify it by projecting certain past experiences into the present. The transferred idea can therefore become conscious before all other possible ideas because it gives satisfaction at the same time to resistance. Again and again, a patient first pushed into consciousness a part of the pathogenic complex that was capable of transference and then defended it with the greatest tenacity. All conflicts must ultimately be fought out on the field of transference; that is the place where all the patient's problems converge as if in one point and join together in a "no man's land between illness and life," an "artificial illness."

In order to achieve a resolution of these transference phenomena, one must understand their relationship to resistance; that, however, is possible only if one decides to distinguish between a "positive" and a "negative" transference. Resistance is served only by negative transference and the offspring of repressed erotic stimulations, which manifest themselves as positive transference. Through interpretation they are made conscious and thus nullified; the other components that are inoffensive and capable of becoming conscious, such as genuine feelings of fondness and attraction, remain the same and ultimately lead the analysis to success. Where transference capability has become essentially negative, there is no more possibility of influence and healing. As a technical rule that is supposed to eliminate the possibility of the patient's being influenced by the facial expression of the analyst, Freud selected the arrangement of having the patient lie on the couch in order to protect against the unnoticed mingling of the transference with ideas that occur to the patient.

With this rule Freud had created an effective instrument for the very purpose of exploiting the "compulsion to repeat" of his patients, in order to overcome their imprisonment to the past and to open up the road into the future. In the effort really to understand the patient, however, he faced the same difficulty as any hermeneutical effort in regard to a text. The transference could no more become the object of the analyst's experience than the unconscious could be the object of observation. The "hermeneutical circle" had to be considered.

The circular structure into which the discovery of transference phenomena necessarily leads is demonstrated by the fact that if one is to maintain the ubiquity of transference—and Freud left no doubt about this—then the analyst also produces a transference to his patient. He too will be provoked by the patient to completely spontaneous and immediate manifestations of feeling, for which Freud coined the term "countertransference." From this finding came two requirements that Freud presented with the stringency of a categorical imperative: First, under no circumstances could the analyst permit himself to respond to the transference feelings of the patient in terms of his own need and emotion, and to act out these feelings together with the patient. In the case of the transference-conditioned infatuation of a patient, he must exact from himself the unpleasant recognition "that the love of the patient is forced by the analytical situation and cannot be ascribed, say, to the good qualities of his person, and that he thus has no reason at all to be proud of such a 'conquest,' as one might call it outside analysis." Hence he must make himself conscious of the fact that transference love stands in service to resistance and from the patient's standpoint is only supposed to serve the goal of maneuvering the analyst out of his role and breaking his authority "through his demotion to the position of lover." "Thus it is certain that he can draw no personal advantage from it." Above all, it was the ethic of the physician that Freud placed over everything here and which restrained any accession to love in regard to the patient. In every case it required of him a renunciation, and that meant an uncompromising inner struggle "against the powers that would draw him away from the analytical level" and have him slip unawares into tender feelings toward the patient. On the other hand, however, this requirement meant that the analyst had to become conscious of his own manifestations of countertransference, in order thus to be able "to hold them down with indifference."

How should the analyst behave in order not to founder in the situation created by transference and countertransference? As stringently as Freud maintained the requirement of renunciation on the part of the analyst, he expected little from verbally making such an outright demand of the patient. The suppression of the patient's desire for love seemed to him as disastrous as accession to it. The way of the analyst is different: ultimately he will indeed have to lead the patient to renunciation also, but by means of interpretation, not by demand.

> One must guard against diverting the love transference, driving it off, or spoiling it for the patient. One refrains equally steadfastly from any reciprocation of the same. One maintains the love transference but treats it as something unreal, as a situation that in therapy is to be passed through, that is to be traced back to its unconscious origins, and that must help to lead the most obscure part of the patient's love life into consciousness and thereby to control.

Thus interpretation represents the way in which, through expanded understanding, the unconscious repression can be replaced by conscious renunciation. The patient thereby learns the conquest of the pleasure principle,

> the renunciation of an available but socially improper satisfaction in favor of a more distant one, perhaps basically more uncertain but impeccable psychologically as well as socially. For the purpose of this conquest the patient is to be led through the early stages of her mental development and in this way acquire the *more than mental freedom* that distinguishes conscious from unconscious mental activity.

We have treated in such detail the rules that Freud established for handling transference and countertransference because in them a central point for all dealings with people becomes visible, the perception that an outright demand can accomplish nothing, or expressed theologically, that the law only brings wrath (Rom. 4:15). In the place of the one-sidedness of order and obedience, Freud put the circular structure of mutual reciprocity, with which the analyst himself takes over the demand for renunciation—taking the place of the patient, so to speak, who is still unable to accept it—until the patient himself, through the effectiveness of interpretations, becomes able to make the renunciation. Freud himself probably did not see with the same acuity as the literature after him what a monstrous requirement he had placed on the analyst himself. We will return to this problem after we have first brought to mind the operation of interpretive technique.

It was Freud's goal to achieve for his patients the greatest amount of freedom from the powers of the past, freedom that could open up for them the horizon of the future. He endeavored to give back to the "ego the control over lost areas of mental life." To that end the patient had to experience his problems "not as a historical affair but as a real power." This happened in transference. Through the seeking-out of the repressed, the uncovering of resistances, and the indication of what is doing the repressing, the conflict of repression is renewed; and because the patient's ego has now become stronger vis-à-vis the childhood conflict situation and the patient has the doctor at his side as helper, the therapeutic effort can hope "to lead the conflict to a better outcome." The resolution of the patient's conflicts and the overcoming of resistances succeed, however, only "if one has given him ideas and expectations that are in agreement with the reality inside him."

How can psychoanalysis fulfill this lofty requirement of really encountering the inner reality of the patient, and what pathways could it follow with its art of interpretation? Their direction can be indicated with three fundamental perceptions.

1. The presupposition of psychoanalytical interpretation is the unshakable certainty of the meaningful coherence of all psychic life. If one took one's partners as seriously as Freud took his patients, they could never become objects of an objective knowledge that sought to comprehend them with the categories of findings already at hand. The inquiry would instead have to be reversed, in the sense, for example, of the position that Schelling took in regard to tradition: "In which direction must our thoughts be expanded in order to be in proportion to the phenomenon?" Thus, in regard to his patients, Freud forbade himself to recur to the "suspicion of

meaninglessness," as the hermeneutics and psychology before him had to a large extent done. For him a psychic experience was, of itself and by definition, meaningful, and he tried to design a theoretical framework of meaning that claimed to comprehend the totality of the person in the past and the present. Yet this could not be achieved once and for all. From the moment he discovered for the first time that the thought processes of a hysterical person did not obey the laws of "logical connection" and that the "existence of secret, hidden, unconscious motives" had to be assumed, the task of interpretation presented itself again and again. As the most important instrument of the psychoanalytical processes, it had to be created anew in each case. This fundamental, historical changeability of the interpretive processes opened ever new horizons of understanding, until Freud finally stood before the residue of the past in the psyche of his patient and had thereby gained even for that psyche an "understandable motivational context."

2. Now, however, in order for the patient to be able to participate in such a meaningful understanding of his behavior and his communications, these first had to be moved a certain distance from him. This happened by means of that function of language that one can call name giving and objectifying. On the basis of indications made by the patient himself, an effort is made, with the aid of the psychoanalytical art of interpretation and through the words of the analyst, to bring the unconscious complex before the consciousness of the patient. As Wolfgang Loch expressed it, "A behavior that is experienced as foreign and frightening is given a name, which 'replaces' it. Thereby something highly significant in itself takes place: by means of name giving one achieves an objectification of a formerly private, unobjective process [and] the previously nameless unknown [moves] into the realm of one's own or another person's accessibility." It was Freud's great discovery that this function of the analytical process received substantial support from the fact that the motives for such name giving do not have to be found anew but through their involvement with the past are already at hand in the psychic nucleus, as it were, and have ages ago found their linguistic expression in myth. Freud demonstrated this evidence at length—probably conditioned by his own biographical experiences—in regard to one mythic motif: for him the Oedipus motif

became the core complex of neuroses. Others extended this point of view to other myths, such as the story of paradise and the tower of Babel. Freud thus learned to relate mythic traditions and pathogenic material to each other and always to understand the one better on the basis of the other.

3. The actual interpretive processes, however, can be made clear only in the reciprocal operation of the hermeneutical circle between the patient and the therapist. If the analyst wants to place at the patient's disposal a psychological explanation as a hypothesis for previously unrelated, adjacent psychic acts and conditions, he can do this only on the basis of his own countertransference, for real perception can consist only in "rediscovering" an object. Where a countertransference does not arise, there can be no analysis, and no analyst can go further than his own complexes and inner resistances permit. Thus through his own "productive prejudices" (in Hans Georg Gadamer's sense) the analyst will develop a prior understanding with which he approaches the material offered, and he confronts the patient with this prior understanding. Now, it is crucial, however, that this prior understanding be verified or rejected by the patient himself; that is, the prejudices and biases of the analyst "must be introduced for the purpose of clarifying meaning, must yield to the purpose of finding meaning, that is, they must at any time be correctable."[8]

Thus Freud, as Ludwig Binswanger remarked, "based hermeneutics first of all on experience." Since psychological hermeneutics must always pay attention to the psychological content of the speaker's utterances, what the analyst perceives directly will become the key to the work of interpretation. Only this "interpretation through the living object" can put life into the ordered material. As a rule this happens especially when sudden processes of understanding on the part of the patient spontaneously betray themselves. Wittgenstein described this process very graphically: "What happens when a person suddenly understands? What are the characteristic psychic phenomena that accompany sudden understanding? 'Now I see!' is one cry; it corresponds to a natural sound, a joyous convulsion." With the perception of such manifest experiences, which can be received only with the help of the analyst's countertransference, the hermeneutical circle, in Kierkegaard's sense, is closed: "The pupil is the reason that the teacher understands himself; the teacher is the reason that the pupil understands himself." The circle swings back to the demand that the analyst must have already understood his countertransference. "When the doctor has understood the 'question,' the 'countertransference' (which indeed always contains a 'demand'), to which the pathological state of the patient is the 'answer,' then he succeeds in finding that interpretive word that opens up for the patient the horizon of understanding for this, his becoming"; and then the words of R. G. Collingwood are borne in mind: "In truth one can understand a text only if one has understood the question to which it is an answer."

With that we come back to the question of what demand is actually made of the analyst with the assignment of this role. When no transference and countertransference can be produced, even interpretation reaches its definitive limits. Therefore Freud excluded "narcissistically structured" psychoses from treatability through psychoanalysis. But does the possibility of psychoanalytic treatment not already reach its limits a lot earlier, namely, when one looks closely—as has frequently happened in the literature after Freud—at the role assigned to the analyst in the interpretive process? Can this really be achieved by a human being?

The fact that Freud had assigned to the analyst in the psychoanalytic process the role of a catalytic agent[9] and at times could hold the position that he "had fully rationalized the situation between us and the patient so that it can be comprehended like a problem in arithmetic"—this had repeatedly brought into play the question of the "mirror function of the analyst." Thus it is regularly imputed to Freud that he held the opinion that the analyst must take it upon himself "for a certain time to transfer no feelings to the other person, . . . to conduct himself like a highly polished mirror surface," that is, like an inanimate object. At this point we must raise the question of whether this does not impose a plainly superhuman requirement. Such feelings of omnipotence on the part of the analyst were certainly foreign to Freud himself. The call for "unlimited transference" that is seen in Christ's profound words to the paralytic, "Your sins are forgiven; stand up and walk," cannot be emulated by psychoanalysis. "Suppose I were to say to a patient, 'I, Professor Sigmund Freud, forgive you your sins.' What humiliation in my case!" Thus also Werner Kemper could only call it a "dispelled illusion" that "analysts as thoroughly analyzed individuals represent a pure, disturbance-free, continually impartial projection surface for the one-sided transference tendencies of the patient." He showed that transference is unavoidably part of being human, and that it also governs the analyst "with his never too 'normalizing' structural characteristics with their specific forms of experience and their corresponding world view." With recourse to Freud's technical rule of steady, free-floating attention, he reproduced Freud's original intention to exploit countertransference precisely as the most important diagnostic instrument, provided that it can be made conscious through definite technical rules and limited in its utterances. This must lead to "our holding our own latent world of impulses so loosely at our disposal that we immediately capture the corresponding utterances of the patient in our own strings as in an instrument tuned to the same pitch."

Hence, what is required is not the omnipotence of a pure mirror attitude but the dialectically paradoxical task of "holding one's own emotions loosely at one's disposal, so that in the interest of the patient they resonate as the most important instrument of perception and yet are constantly held in check, 'frustrated,' so that they do not enter uncontrolled into the emotional activity of the patient." Even this represents, according to Kemper, a demand that sometimes goes to the limits of human capability, but it is indeed precisely this human weakness that—clearly recognized and properly evaluated—is beneficial to the analytical work.

Wolfgang Loch finally raised these relationships to methodological clarity. For him also it was true that countertransference is only a force that destroys analytical power when it "does its mischief in the dark." What distinguishes the analyst from the patient is the use he makes of his emotional reactions in order to shape his countertransference into a perceiving apparatus that comprehends the behavior and reaction of the patient as being evoked through countertransference. The difficulty consists in the ambivalence with which he requires countertransference on the one hand "to be tuned for general understanding" and on the other to be repeatedly "suspended . . . in order to interpret to the patient his behavior." But even here it is demonstrated that "we win our analytical match

98

as a person and thereby let the partner be a person when we miss the ideal by a hairbreadth, for absolute omnipotence excludes the autonomy of the other person. We must be missing at some point so that the other person can continue alone."

Logically thinking through to the end the technical rules of psychoanalysis leads thus into dimensions that go beyond this narrow framework. At stake is the quest for the deepest ground of human existence. Loch described it elsewhere:

> Being able to turn loose is the most spiritual reason for the abstinence of which the analyst must be capable. He must endure being alone in this sense, which he can only do if he can be alone without becoming lonely; for loneliness experienced as abandonment and isolation is already a psychopathological phenomenon that impedes or prevents understanding, to say nothing of turning loose. The analyst is protected from pathogenic "primary loneliness" only if his being alone is always performed with confidence, with that "primal trust" that bears every self-projection into the future.

Thus it may be clear that a psychoanalytical hermeneutic that takes itself seriously cannot stop with the "comprehensibility of a problem in arithmetic" but leads from its presuppositions to problems very similar to those of theological hermeneutics. Properly understood, psychoanalysis does not lead into the "closed system" of a view of humanity defined and fixed once and for all but rather reveals precisely the unremitting "ambiguities" of real life which leave room for the interpretation of human existence in faith. Thus Freud did not leave the conditionalities of human life standing as a mystery no longer to be probed; on the contrary, he expanded by a good bit the horizons of understanding.

LANGUAGE AND HISTORICAL DYNAMICS

Freud had introduced language as a means of therapy into the science of healing. He followed the flow of language, which does not permit the patient to be understood as an object to be influenced, and thereby arrived at the dialogical structure of hermeneutical understanding. This also opened up for him a completely new view of illness itself that is deeply and firmly rooted in language. Very early Freud made the curious discovery that hysterical patients develop an extremely odd relationship to certain linguistic formulations that we understand as symbolic: they understand them literally. By taking the "linguistic expression literally," by perceiving as a real state of affairs the "slap in the face" or the "stab in the back" of an offending statement, they are not practicing a humorous misuse but rather are simply giving life "once again to those feelings to which the linguistic expression owes its validity." The neurotic is thus not able to take the linguistic formulations that are present in his memory and hold them at a critical distance, as it were, through an assessment of their symbolic character; they are understood literally and thereby receive a renewed reality, which in the case of the hysterical person is transferred directly into the body. Whoever is continually ill treated verbally will really become ill; whoever continually has to stomach things will develop real stomach conditions; whoever is under the pressure of anxiety will also feel real pressure in the chest; and so forth. Thus the neurotic actually becomes ill through his interaction with the language, which remains in the form of mnemonic symbols. Instead of having these mnemonic symbols at his disposal and being able to give them linguistic expression and to be responsible for them, he realizes them in his body and becomes "possessed" by them.

Freud researched intensively the question of how such deviant linguistic behavior can come about, and he reached the following explanation. In his studies on dreams he became convinced that every person harbors in his own soul a psychic "system" that does not correspond to the linguistic and conceptual conventions of the present. In this system conceptual laws such as the principle of contradiction are not valid; in it there are no relationships to time and number; in it there reigns a conceptual and linguistic identity between things that are linked symbolically today. Freud called it an "archaic system of expression," because outside of dreams he saw its validity also in myths, fairy tales, sagas, figures of speech, proverbs, and jokes. In a dream as well as in neurosis, mental activity shows a regressive tendency—and indeed in three respects: topically, in that it takes refuge in the unconscious part of the psychic system; temporally, in that it gives new life to old formulations; and formally, in that it makes use of primitive modes of expression. Dreaming is thus regression to the earliest relationships of the dreamer, behind whose individual childhood an insight opens up into the phylogenetic childhood, into the development of the human race in general. Through the analysis of dreams one can thus achieve knowledge of the archaic heritage of humankind, which Freud could call nothing other than the "mentally innate."[10] What so-called dreamwork accomplishes, therefore, is the regressive treatment of thoughts which connects the latent dream ideas to the archaic system of expression, opens a regressive path for the stimulus, and thus transforms the idea back into the sensuous picture from which it originally came.

Now, on the basis of this model gained from dreams, the origination of neurotic symptoms can also be interpreted. In the beginning Freud assumed that it always had to be a real experience whose renewed life as a memory must have a traumatic effect as soon as it is connected, along the regressive path, to the archaic system of expression. Yet experience showed that this could also be the case with fantasy, which exhibited an extremely significant relationship to time. Fantasy floats, as it were, among the three temporal elements of our imagination:

> Mental activity is linked to a current impression, a cause in the present, which is capable of arousing one of the great desires of the person; it reaches back from there to the memory of an early, usually infantile experience in which that desire was fulfilled; and now it creates a situation connected to the future, which presents itself as the fulfillment of that desire.

The decisive question now is whether the fantasy assumes a predominantly regressive character, whether it continues to be alienated from reality through a regression into the infantile: then the result is neurosis. It is represented in our time, according to Freud, by the cloister, "into which all of those persons customarily withdrew whom life had disappointed or who felt that they were too weak for life." Fantasy can, however, also strike out in a progressive direction; that is, it can endeavor through work to be transformed into reality. Then the result may be "victorious wish fantasies" that reestablish their connection with reality and overcome the power of the neurosis.

Neurotic illness is thus placed into a historical context. The neurotic is incapable of feeling himself a historical being. Freud saw plainly as a criterion for differential diagnosis the fact that the neurotic is incapable of giving an ordered presentation of his life's history. The ill suffer from memories that have been repressed and are no longer accessible. Therefore they cannot be open to the future but must project the past into the future in a constant "compulsion to repeat." They have become ahistorical. The symptom is the mnemonic symbol of traumatic impressions and fantasies that have fallen into the whirlpool of regression. The archaic system of expression has left its stamp on them; they are, so to speak, "cut out" of the time continuum; a certain period of time has gained a special quality, has become the traumatizing "kairos," and in ever new editions completely rules experience and emotions.[11] Everything new that appears in the life of such a person must be experienced as alien and hostile; it cannot be enjoyably rediscovered in one's own self, and there can be no anamnesis, because the remnants of the past, including the phylogenetic inheritance, are cut off and inaccessible. Instead of this, only the opposite can occur: the new is adulterated into the old, since the latter is unconsciously projected into the present and the future.

Now, it is the task of psychoanalytic healing to remove this amnesia. "When all the gaps in memory are filled, when all the enigmatic affects of psychic life are explained, the continuation of suffering is impossible." This can happen, however, only when a new "kairos," a special, meaningful time, is experienced in the life of the patient. Such are the hours of treatment, in which—through the linguistic function of interpretation in transference—the regressive direction gradually changes into a progressive one, the time continuum is reestablished, and the inner processes in the ego are accorded the quality of consciousness. The direction can become progressive only if what is repressed is "recognized as past, devalued, and deprived of its investment of emotional energy," that is, if through analytical work unconscious ideas become conscious. The function of language hence turns to its most characteristic essence: to liberate. But what is liberated? Freud could only answer, love. "Every psychoanalytic treatment is an attempt to liberate repressed love, which has found a miserable, compromising escape in a symptom." Only love is in a position to undertake those changes in reality that will prevent the contradiction between desire and the world encountered outside from becoming a conflict situation that is so depressing and leads to regression.

Perhaps it will no longer be surprising now if we assert that parallels can be drawn between the therapeutic task that Freud set with the introduction of language into the science of healing and the efforts of contemporary theology to orient the task of proclamation toward language. We would merely like to call attention to several of these parallels in the hermeneutics of Ernst Fuchs.

With Fuchs hermeneutics presses energetically into the "sphere of experience"; if for him it is a matter of "not adhering to the imaginary distinction between theory and practice," he affirms that "the ontic [*existentiell*] interpretation is the criterion for understanding in the existential [*existential*] interpretation." Thus is the Bultmannian prior understanding developed into hermeneutical principle. It is supposed "to gain dominion over the process of understanding" by showing what the "power and truth of a process lend" to understanding in general and how this process gets into motion. It is, so to speak, what one holds out to a text (or on the other hand, to a person), in order to elicit from it what it has to say; just as when one wants to understand a cat, one has only to provide it with a mouse. In regard to the New Testament it is the knowledge that I cannot keep up the quest for myself, and hence the "moral gravity of the exegete" (Fuchs). This truthfulness is the only ontic presupposition, and hence today the hermeneutical principle for the exegesis of the New Testament. Now, the truth that could make humankind understandable must be sought where a person relates himself to himself. "If you want to understand him, you must be able to give him freedom; then freedom would be the hermeneutical principle of humanity."

But where is the place that this moral gravity might be found and a person could, so to speak, be handed his freedom? It can only be language that brings this about. Language installs us in the realm of our existence which defines our life; therefore, being originates from language. Nothing is real until it can be made present by putting it into language, and thus reality can be regarded as only a "category" of language. It appears only when the rules of language are followed, so that language and world can become synonyms. Thus in the realm of theology, hermeneutics is the "grammar of faith."

Now, the most significant step in the hermeneutics of Fuchs, however, is that he developed language and expanded its understanding on two sides: in the direction of time and in the direction of love. If reality can be understood only as a category of language, then language no longer interprets faith on the horizon of reality "but on the horizon of time itself and reveals time to us as the actual 'place' of existence before God." If the essence of language is based on the possibility of remembering, then the ground of our existence becomes time, and the existential interpretation inquires of history how a person deals with time. Here, in Fuchs's opinion, Heidegger's efforts to interpret time as the possibility of itself that lies in existence must run aground as soon as interpretation moves over to the gospel, for being is indeed ontically time yet not the time lying within us but rather the very time taken from us. The Bultmannian concept of "desecularization" and the self-surrender demanded by Jesus are now interpreted as the "giving-up of the attempt to control time as the origin of existence"; this means, however, that it depends on whether a person intends to understand his time out of the power of the future or "out of the empty past." This understanding of time comes, however, from the truth of language. Indeed, language simply announces what it is time for, and the proclamation of Jesus is the "announcement of time itself, the new time of God's kingdom." Also, by its nature, time is not a "standard of measurement" but rather time for something; what is essential to it is its sharpening of the distinction between times. Faith is rid of the past; it is free from it, for in Jesus it came about that the past surrendered its power to the future.

Now, with Jesus, however, in terms of content, what is the time announced for? Answer: It is the time for love, for "the nature of language is its pull toward love, out of love." It lives in its most characteristic ground "from that yes that is the word above all words. . . . In the beginning was the yes, and the yes was love, and love was the yes." Language thus expresses the experience of love, for it actually never says no; it knows only the yes, and we perceive the "inner pull of language as the pull of God's word." Is language therefore divine? This, in all seriousness, is the question that moves Fuchs; and for Christian existence the one directive can be given: "First you shall live. . . . And in your life you shall give attention to the experiences you have with love. . . . Love guarantees itself. Whoever has this experience believes . . . for now one inserts in place of the word 'love' the word 'God.'"

Yet where is the picture of a person realized who lives thus and "wants to be nothing for himself"? Answer: In the historical Jesus, for "the question that is called Jesus must be asked anew of a person by exposing the natural and historical conditions of his origin." Jesus wanted to love his neighbor; if I want that too, then I want the same thing he did. The miracle that is called Jesus consists in the fact that he was nothing for himself and he himself already behaved as a new person. His coming again is the talk of "liberating freedom," and faith prepares itself for this "restricting and releasing power of freedom." Thus, according to its structure, faith in Jesus is love, and the historical Jesus becomes our helper so that we may understand, for existential interpretation adds to the text this helper who leads us into the world of the text. Fuchs's hermeneutics have thus brought together life, love, language, and faith into a square, in the sense of the later Heidegger, and contributed to a widening of the Bultmannian "bottleneck."

Therefore, one can only acknowledge with deep gratitude Fuchs's often more intuitively than systematically executed endeavors toward a concretization of the hermeneutical question. His American friends have found that he should go even further in his development of the human side, that all of the semantically significant words have been distilled out of his language, that he stubbornly refuses to circumscribe the content of faith, and that he offers an inadequate anthropology. Could this impression perhaps be traced back to the fact that Fuchs has not completely freed himself from the intellectualistically limiting interpretation of Heidegger that can see the basic fact of human existence—that one is withdrawn from oneself—only in the sense of an isolated self-understanding? One's being withdrawn from oneself then becomes a being invisible to oneself, a being hidden from oneself, a standing vis-à-vis oneself as a mystery, with which the "mystery of the presence of God" stands in a corresponding relationship, so that we come to the curious statement that "God has the tightest hold on us precisely

105

not in our consciousness, and also not in the explorable subconscious, but in the unconscious."

Can one, however, really turn God into a phenomenon of the unconscious at a time when increasing consciousness seems to us to have become the destiny and, indeed, plainly the mandate of Christianity? We would not like to stop with this information and silently revere the "mystery of immediacy," before which our thinking has previously failed. If the existential interpretation in no way excludes psychological considerations but, on the contrary, paves the way for them, it should no doubt also be subjected to the challenge of asking itself whether all that Fuchs presents in so model a fashion as the description of Christian existence—deliverance from the past and into the future, liberation from all enigmas to an unambiguous exposition of existence in love, and so forth—whether all of this is not also to be found similarly in Freud.

With psychoanalysis Freud did not want to create an unbiased scientific investigation; his passion was not for proof but for change. He wanted to liberate "all energies that today are distorted in the production of neurotic symptoms in the service of a fantasy world isolated from reality" and instead to use them "to help strengthen the cry for those changes in our culture that are the only ones in which we can see salvation for posterity." Psychoanalysis is thus expanded to social criticism and, in this expansion, also to religious criticism. We believe that it would also be rewarding to give it the attention of a critical dialogue. We can also expect of this dialogue that it could stimulate and enrich present-day theological reflection. As Freud himself asked, Just why should the success that therapy can have with the individual not also be achieved with the masses?

5

THE APPLICATION

Freud's Views on Religion

At an advanced age Freud himself felt that the development of psychoanalysis as a therapeutic method for the healing of individual people was merely a prelude to his actual life's vocation. He designated as his "life's triumph" the fact that from a certain time on he had rediscovered the initial direction of his early years, which consisted in the overpowering need "to understand something of the puzzles of the world and perhaps even to contribute something to their solution." From this standpoint he could call his career—which led him through broad areas of the natural sciences, medicine, and psychotherapy—a detour to the actual goal, the "cultural problems." For him, however, that meant that, beginning with one turning point in his thinking, he gave "free reign to the long-suppressed inclination toward speculation," that after that time he could strive for the "dissolution of conventional cultural certainties." He devoted a large part of his life's work to "destroying his own and humanity's illusions," he wanted nothing more than "to do research, solve puzzles, discover a little bit of truth,"[1] and he selected for himself as his final area of inquiry the theme of death. In the process of making this long-desired application of psychoanalytic findings and perceptions to culture, Freud encountered a power that he experienced only as very intimately bound to this culture itself: the power of religious concepts and precepts. Therefore, when Freud decided on an intensive interaction with religion, he did so—as David Riesman ("Freud and

Psychoanalysis") convincingly sets forth—to a large extent not in the role of the attacker but in the role of the attacked. In Freud's conceptual world it was also supposed to be—according to an apt formulation by J. Klauber—the task of religion to reconcile the masses with culture, and humankind with nature. In Freud's opinion, the contemporary expressions of religion were only to an inadequate extent equal to this task. He approached religion with the critical probe of psychoanalytic perceptions and had to prepare himself at the same time for the angry protests of the representatives of religion and other contemporaries.

When one could no longer dispute very well the successes of the Freudian method in the clinical area,[2] the conflict began at other points. Thus, issue was taken both with Freud's attempt to clarify and interpret his psychological findings philosophically[3] and with the transformation of the therapeutic method into a psychology that had something to say about other areas of social phenomena.[4] Since Freud let it be known that he himself was a stranger to religious experience, some felt that he must also be deprived of the ability to understand it.

There is now, however, a strong theological current, especially in American Protestantism,[5] that asserts that one can use to advantage certain Freudian thought processes for the purpose of Christian apologetics. Freud's emphasis on anxiety and his pessimism in regard to the future of the human race are seen as the result of an anthropology that can only grow in the soil of concepts like those shaped within the Christian tradition in the doctrine of original sin.[6] Above all, however, Freud deposed reason, emphasized the irrational, and placed on the throne a certain mystical attitude. As decisively as Freud guarded against letting himself be accused of irrationality, he approached just as intently, on the other hand, positions that are otherwise known only in mysticism.[7] It is on the *via negationis* that the God-seeker discovers that not everything he finds is God.[8] Thus one could say with exaggeration that God is present in Freud's reflections in the mode of absence or, in his own language, as a phenomenon of repression.[9] What Novalis said of Spinoza, that he was "God-intoxicated" can perhaps also be said of Freud. In any case, in the second half of his life he struggled continually, in ever new approaches, with the phenomenon of religion.

In the theological dialogue with Freud, we must nevertheless reject as methodologically inadequate the idea of permitting those parts of his thinking that fit into our dogmatic plans while rejecting as impermissible trespasses others that serve a religious-critical function. Two things must, of course, be kept in mind if one wants to look more closely at Freud's ideas on religion:

1. Freud's analyses of religion do not allow themselves to be harmonized into a unified and homogeneous presentation of the topic. One can do them justice to some extent only if one considers them in their historical development.

2. Freud neither entered into a discussion with contemporary theology nor tried to aim an attack at those things which, as "religious experience," are not subject to normal verification.[10] His criticism of religion was always directed against only the "outward forms of religion"—against "what the common man understands by religion"—and only with this did he want to take issue. He was interested in religious rules and rites, in the formations of faith within our society. His critical inquiries into these may, therefore, be of significance primarily for the practical disciplines of theology.

RELIGION AND NEUROSIS

Freud's first intensive interaction with religious phenomena probably occurred in the year 1897 at the time of his self-analysis, on which he faithfully reported to his friend Wilhelm Fliess. From these letters we learn that in the effort to refresh memories of early childhood, Freud became conscious of two different types of piety with which he had been brought into contact in this early period. There were on the one hand the wisdom teachings of the Jewish tradition that were transmitted to him by his father, who himself came from the Hasidic milieu, and which were passed on primarily through the reading of Holy Scripture.[11] On the other hand, Freud reported that the nursemaid of his first years of life, who was Catholic, had taken him into every church[12] and that he had preached when he came home. The early childhood formation of the picture of religion that developed within Freud can thus be traced back to two fundamental types: a more masculine, intellectually defined type from paternal tradition and a more intensely feminine, emotionally shaped type from Catholic folk piety. Yet it can be easily observed that in the course of his self-analysis Freud was able to achieve an astonishingly far-reaching consciousness in his interaction with the paternal side, and the feminine realm remained completely closed to him for a disproportionately long time.[13] The analysis of this problem given by Hjalmar Sundén in disagreement with Andrew Salter (*The Case against Psychoanalysis*) makes it probable that in Freud's unconscious ideas, the Catholic type of piety was connected with femininity in general and suffered a more rigorous repression than the more intensely rationalistic type of the paternal religion.[14] Therein may lie a contribution to the answer to the question of why in Freud's ideas on religion there is such an unambiguous and one-sided predominance of the father problem.[15]

The first published results of Freud's disagreement with religion came in a work from the year 1907, in which he called attention to the parallel between the compulsive actions of neurotics and the practice of religion. What Freud's critics largely overlooked is the fact that this parallel is a very limited one; one must also see the "glaring" differences. Compulsive neurosis in every case involves but a single and uniform rite, but greater multiplicity reigns in the case of religion; a public character is appropriate to the latter, but the former is played out completely in secret. Neurotic symptoms are meaningless to the one who is subjected to them; religious activities are intended to be meaningful and symbolic. Therefore Freud could call compulsive neurosis the half comic, half tragic distortion of a private religion. As long as the individual believer is conscious of the meaning and symbol content of a ceremony, he does not, in Freud's view, stand on common ground with the neurotic. That does not become the case until the pious one ceases to inquire at all about the meaning of religious actions. Now, to be sure, Freud believed that he could assert, in an impermissible generalization, that the motives that push one toward the practice of religion are to the same degree unknown to all believers and are always represented in consciousness by pretended motives. He admitted, of course, that "sporadically started reforms" repeatedly attempt a reestablishment of the original structure, but apparently their effectiveness seemed to him not to be especially impressive.

On the other hand, Freud observed with amazement that religion was obviously in a position to "tame" sexual strivings in that it offered "sublimation and solid mooring" through the opening up of social relationships, and thus provided fellowship. His reason recognized this victory of religion over instinctual forces, but his rationalistic understanding could feel no joy over the victory. He maintained that turning oneself over to the divinity might not be the only way in which one could free oneself "from the control of evil, socially harmful instincts."

Above all, he was noticeably disturbed by the observation that neuroses apparently increase to the extent that the determining influence of religion is diminished. If the number of neurotics is so clearly increasing, if more and more people have to flee into the "caricature of a private religion," then there must also be something wrong with the life styles of religion that it can no longer make its contribution to the socialization of humanity. He believed that the fault had to be seen in the fact that there was a discrepancy between the stage of maturity of humankind as a whole and the life styles of faith, which had fallen into the whirlpool of regression. He saw in them a "regressive renewal of infantile protective powers" and finally came to the conclusion that the personal God is *"psychologically* nothing more than an elevated father." Whoever is religious is spared the development of an individual neurosis; therefore, religion is regarded psychologically as nothing but a "universal compulsive neurosis."

On the trail of a thus conceived father problem in religious phenomena, Freud then went further. The trail led him, while on vacation in Tirol in the year 1911,[16] to intensive reflection on the curious phenomenon that the erected likenesses of the crucified One, in especially large numbers there, were designated as "Lord Gods." This melding of the Father and the crucified One seemed to him to rest on a religious need that seemed to satisfy a desire for the diminution of the Father. Thus the Oedipus complex became for him the central problem of the "Lord God" figures in Tirol.

We remain convinced that the pivotal point for Freud's interest in the forms of religious phenomena consists in the observation that in religion are cultivated modes of behavior that in the life of the individual must be called pathological: the passing-down of cultic forms whose content in meaning and symbol is no longer accessible to the individual, and the use of religious symbols for the satisfaction of psychic needs such as the diminution of the Father. The idea that in these forms of religious phenomena there might also lie a misuse of the actual content of the faith was a consideration that Freud stubbornly resisted. For him the external forms of religious life constituted at the same time its nature, which could only be regarded as absolutely ahistorical. As if it were dogma, he held fast to the assertion that religion was not capable of further development. In all essential parts it was complete; if it was a mistake, it must remain so forever. Thus for Freud access to an inner reform of the structure of faith remained cut off. Since, however, in individual therapy he succeeded in liberating from compulsions by making them conscious, he thought that the same success must also occur with the masses. He thus tried to subject the religious phenomenon to the same conditions for understanding as neurosis and endeavored thus in ever new approaches to penetrate to the real core of the problem.

RELIGION AND THE MYTH OF ORIGIN

Freud's ability to understand an aspect of religious behavior modes better with the help of neurosis theory encouraged him to extend this method into other areas also. He learned to unite conceptual structures of the past with phenomena of the unconscious that are still alive in the present in a circle of mutual understanding, and to relate them to each other. This possibility stands or falls, however, with a certain prior historical-philosophical judgment that was first pointed out by Vico and adopted relatively early by Freud in his work, namely, that ontogeny can be regarded as a recapitulation of phylogeny. Thus the conceptual structures that rule early childhood—the point of origin of all neurotic conflicts—throw a new light on the early period of human intellectual history and vice versa. Because in early childhood there is an unusually great openness to the realm of the unconscious, in a form that no longer exists later on, Freud felt the conclusion could be allowed that this was also true of early human history. The transcendence of the mythological conception of the world revealed itself to him as the transcendence of unconscious mental activity, which set before science the task of transforming that transcendent reality into a psychology of the unconscious—of transposing metaphysics into metapsychology. With this, early human history moved into the center of Freud's interest.

Now, there were two phenomena that he saw active in present-day culture for which, in his work *Totem und Tabu* (Totem and taboo), he sought clarification in early human history. The first was the strange fact that the people of our civilization accept ethical precepts, such as Kant's categorical imperative, which can work in a compulsory fashion and for which every conscious motivation is rejected. The second was the profound feeling of guilt that is encountered in every person, independent of individual life history, and is obviously a part of human existence; and this deeply puzzled Freud. He searched for the early stages of these two modes of behavior that accorded so poorly with the Enlightenment thinking of his time and came upon the prescriptive taboos and the totemism of primitive tribes, which at that very time were being heavily researched.

Freud then endeavored to demonstrate that the prescriptive taboos of primitives exhibited the same structure as the categorical imperative. They "are without any foundation; they are of unknown origin; incomprehensible to us, they seem to be a matter of course for those who are under their sovereignty." Freud, however, wanted to shed some light on the unknown origin of these categorical prohibitions. To that end he was again served by reaching back to childhood, which is accessible to psychological observation. Here it is especially the developmental conditions of the conscience that are of interest. Freud defined the conscience as the "inner perception of the rejection of certain stimulations of desire persisting in us . . . This rejection does not need to appeal to anything else; it is certain of its own self." On the basis of his observations, however, Freud could not regard this inner perception as an innate human characteristic; it first arises, rather, out of very definite human relations in the area of an emotional condition specific to childhood, namely, ambivalence. It consists essentially in the simultaneous presence of both positive and negative emotional relationships with the father. The positive feelings are used to identify with the father, to install his requirements as a separate level of the ego, the so-called superego; the negative feelings, on the other hand, give this superego that harsh, despotic, and often downright cruel trait that knows no reason why.

Freud's interpretation of taboo as the result of the ambivalence conflict convinced even skeptical critics. But he was blamed all the more for the reconstruction of a "powerful primal father" whom he immediately made the central figure of his totem theory.

Here too an observation from child therapy yielded him the key to understanding. He gained it in the analysis of "little Hans," the findings of which he regarded as exemplary for childhood in general. It proved here that the object of anxiety of an animal phobia was adopted as a substitute for the feared father, and that most childhood animal phobias obviously operate in this way. For Freud one of the main puzzles of totemic religion was in this way explained: why, that is, a certain kind of animal was considered holy by a particular clan in primitive society, enjoyed highest honor, yet was slaughtered once a year and consumed by cult members in a solemn meal. For Freud there could be no doubt that the totem animal was to be interpreted as a transference substitute for the father, and indeed for a prehistoric, powerful, primal horde father, whose form he conceived under Darwin's inspiration. The sons had risen up against him and killed him. The guilty traces of the memory of this bloody deed led them later to reincarnate him in an atonement-offering cult. "The totemic religion came forth out of the guilt consciousness of the sons as an attempt to assuage this feeling and propitiate the injured father through belated obedience. . . . They made it a duty again and again to repeat anew the crime of patricide in the sacrifice of the totem animal."

Although Freud believed one must resist the temptation "to derive something so complicated as religion from one single origin," he asserted even so—in an impermissible generalization[17]—that all religions prove to be attempts to solve the same problem, namely, to give an answer to the feeling of guilt in regard to the primal father. In this way he extended the lines of his theory even into the realm of the Christian faith. In the figure and work of Jesus Christ he saw a way to allay consciousness of guilt: "He went forth and sacrificed his own life and thereby redeemed his brothers from original sin." He could see even the Christian Eucharist exclusively from the totemistic viewpoint as a "fresh elimination of the father, a repetition of the atoning deed."

Freud's *Totem und Tabu* provoked sharp objection and harsh rejection. There are but few voices who deem the historical and psychological bases on which the hypothesis of the primal horde is built to be solid enough to give it real support. The most frequently raised objection contends that with the attempt to reconstruct the happenings of a prehistoric primal horde, with which Freud so fundamentally broke out of the conceptual scheme of a logical positivist, he succumbed to the very thinking that he wanted to overcome. It is historical thinking that is conceived on the basis of the myth of origin and asserts temporal priority where it wants to grant authority to something and thus makes the past the master of the present. A certain event at the beginning of history becomes decisive for everything that follows. When the attempt thus to explain and interpret history is combined with the technical error of projecting current social conditions—namely, a patriarchal structure—back onto all original groupings, this provokes the objection of the sociologists especially.

In the face of this criticism, however, one must ask whether it was ever Freud's intention to reconstruct humanity's past as historical reality! Among the people who are thoroughly knowledgeable of the Freudian conceptual world, there are those who believe that this question must be answered with an unequivocal no. Thus Klauber calls the basic conceptions of *Totem und Tabu* pure "spectacle," and Ludwig Binswanger sees in them merely an "idea" that meets the demands of natural scientific research but that does not undertake an outline of the "origin and beginnings of human history." Freud's own statements on this problem are ambiguous. On the one hand, he knew as well as his critics that nowhere had the Darwinian primal horde become the object of observation. On the other hand, at the close of his investigation, in which he discussed the question of whether—as in childhood and in neurosis—the mere impulse of hostility toward the father had not been sufficient to produce the moral reaction, he answered both hastily and defiantly, "Not at all! In the beginning was the deed!" And thus in a self-ironic fashion he signaled his apparent lack of interest in thinking the problem through logically to the end.

For our purposes, the following observation will suffice. In *Totem und Tabu* Freud was already able to present convincingly the question of the binding force of ethical demands and the problem of guilt as the basic givens of human existence. His statements acquire their religious-critical pointedness through the perception that, in view of the present spiritual situation, neither can a common binding force be claimed by an ethical demand that rests on a taboo no longer to be questioned nor can a rite correctly repeated in a totemic manner solve the problem of guilt. This point will be developed more fully in the next chapter.

RELIGION AS ILLUSION

How little Freud was satisfied by his previous studies in the psychology of religion is shown by the fact that at an advanced age he turned again to the problem, this time with a new point of departure. Of course, it was still the psychological laws of development in childhood that were supposed to provide him with the key to understanding, but now he saw them from another viewpoint, which he had acquired by reaching back to an important basic finding of the *Traumdeutung* (The interpretation of dreams). In this work he had identified "wish fulfillment" as the actual moving force of dream formation and later appended the thesis that the same process governs childhood attempts to master life, that is, "to overcome the world of senses in which we are placed by means of the world of wishes." On this foundation he developed the interpretation of human existence as the possibility either of deciding for this "pleasure principle"—that is, remaining imprisoned by the dominance of wishes—or of moving forward to the "reality principle" and getting involved with the real world. The path of human maturation is described as the path of the progressive restriction of the pleasure principle in favor of the reality principle. In dreams, an adult is also allowed a brief return to the pleasure principle's world of wishes, yet if this reaches over into the waking world, if one steadfastly refuses to grow up, one succumbs necessarily to the pathological symptoms of neurosis.

These considerations were now applied by Freud to the realm of religion. He recognized very astutely that assertions of faith can be called truth only in a "higher sense," and that the *credo quia absur-dum* is interesting only as a personal confession of faith. Since the "common man," however, knows only one truth and since truth is as little capable of gradation as is death, he must of necessity mis-understand truth as information about a segment of reality. Thus for Freud assertions of faith fall into the realm of what he calls "illusion." What does he mean by that term? First, it designates the opposite of the "results of experience" and the "final outcome of thought." One thing must be observed, however: "An illusion is not the same thing as an error; it is also not necessarily an error." For it, "derivation from human wishes remains characteristic." By no means, however, does it follow that an illusion has to be false, "that is, unrealizable or in contradiction with reality." Just as the tenets of religion are unprovable, so also are they irrefutable. "We still know too little to give them a closer critical examination." He could see in them merely the fulfillment of the "oldest, strongest, most urgent wishes of humankind." In the realm of religion everything seemed to him to be "just as we wish it." In it humanity belongs more to the pleasure principle than to the reality principle. Against this orien-tation with its "temptations," however, Freud harbored extreme misgivings, because in it he had to fear a propensity to infantile behavior. He emphatically proclaimed, "A human being cannot forever remain a child!" "Experience teaches us that the world is no nursery." He demanded "education to reality."

For Freud, however, this meant withdrawing from the expecta-tions of the next world and concentrating all newly liberated pow-ers on earthly life, for when a culture like the so-called Christian one cannot get along without the satisfaction of a number of people having as a presupposition the oppression of others—perhaps of the majority—it may not have very good prospects of continuing to survive, nor does it deserve to. Thus even the turning-away from religion will be achieved with the predestined implacability of a growth process.

Yet what is the nature of that reality to which Freud wanted to educate? What did he want to put in the place of religious illusions? His reality, into which a person must send himself in "rational resig-nation," offers neither edification nor happiness. "The intention that people are to be happy is not provided for in the plan of creation." Even the "extraordinary progress in the natural sciences . . . has not raised the level of satisfaction of desires" nor made people happier. Also, the hope of a continuous and progressive humanization of human relationships cannot hold its own against reality: "The ideal situation would be a community of people who have subjected their instinctual life to the dictatorship of reason, . . . but that, in all probability, is a utopian hope," for even in the people of today, purely rational motives can do little against passionate impulses. With a certain prophetic persistence, Freud felt himself obligated to present human reality as the "innate inclination of people toward evil, aggression, destruction, and thus also toward cruelty," even if the "dear little children" did not want to hear it.

Over the nice-sounding humanitarian phrases with which many contemporaries tried to manage life, Freud emptied the bowl of his bitter scorn: "The human being has become, so to speak, a kind of prosthesis-god, rather magnificent when he puts on all his auxiliary organs, but they have not become integrated with him and occasionally still leave a lot for him to do." The quintessence remains: "Dark, unfeeling, and unloving powers determine human destiny." Freud attempted to overcome religious infantilism in favor of impersonal reality, a "being without a face, namely, nature." To a faith that stands before such dark powers with the readiness to submit itself to the unsearchable ways of God, Freud summarily denied its qualification as a religion.

> The feeling of human insignificance and impotence by itself does not constitute the essence of religion, but rather the next step, the reaction thereto, which seeks a remedy for this feeling. Whoever goes no further, whoever is humbly satisfied with the insignificant role of humanity in this big world, is rather irreligious in the truest sense of the word.

With his interpretation of certain religious phenomena—which are oriented toward wishful thinking and thus belong to the pleasure principle—as an immature stage of human development, and thus with the almost prophetic pathos of his demand for an orientation toward reality and for finally becoming mature, Freud faced the problem of the historicity of human existence. His orientation toward reality focused with extreme sharpness on the given temporal situation, which he outlined in the last sentences of his *Unbehagen in der Kultur* (Civilization and its discontents):

> The fateful question for the human race, it seems to me, is whether and to what extent in its cultural development it will succeed in mastering the disruption of communal life by human drives toward aggression and self-destruction. People have now reached the point in controlling the forces of nature where, with the help of these forces, they can easily destroy one another down to the last human being. They know that, and this is the reason for a good bit of their unrest, their unhappiness, their mood of anxiety. And now it can be expected that the other of the two "heavenly powers," the eternal eros, will make an effort to assert itself in the struggle with its likewise immortal opponent. But who can predict the result and outcome?

With this question the whole development of culture received a new interpretation. Its meaning can be seen neither in a continuous upward development nor in an eternal recurrence of the same events but rather in the "struggle between eros and death, life and the destruction instinct," which Freud now called the "essential content of life itself." Thus for him love became a "life goal completely independent from science," to which he henceforth felt himself obligated with his life's work and which he tried to comprehend under the caption "healing through love." For him culture became—and with this he also formulated an important point of departure in his criticism of religion—a "process in service to eros, which wants to gather together individual human persons into the great unity of humankind. Why this must happen, we do not know."

The "essentially negative assessment" to which Freud subjected religion in the phase of his development in which he wrote *Die Zukunft einer Illusion* (The future of an illusion) soon appeared inadequate even to Freud himself. Shortly after the publication of this book, which he had written with clearly polemical intent, he wrote to Sandor Ferenczi, "Now it seems childish to me already; basically I think something else. Analytically I consider it weak, and as a confession of faith, inappropriate." Later he himself was able to understand critically that in regard to religion he had created a phantom for the purpose of an expeditious demonstration and in order to get the phenomenon itself out of the way.

In any case, he had not sought, as critics charged, in "monocausalistic fashion" within the "magic circle of a nothing-but-science" to trace the social effect of religion back to nothing more than the "lack of discipline of individual wishful thinking." Freud himself called the contribution of psychoanalysis to religious criticism on the basis of infantile wishful thinking only an indication of the possible origins of religious behavior in childlike helplessness and a warning against a continuation of such wishes and needs into mature life. He thus brought to expression the essential elements that characterize the situation in which theology today must think and speak, and thus forced theologians to an ever-renewed self-critical reflection on the reality of their theology. In his search for the truth content of religion, Freud himself, even in his old age, took some essential steps into the realm that he himself designated with the key word "historical reality."

RELIGION AS HISTORICAL TRUTH

Freud had already written in *Die Zukunft einer Illusion,* "We now notice that the treasury of religious concepts contains not only the fulfillment of wishes but also significant historical reminiscences. . . . Thus religious doctrine imparts to us historical truth." Fascinated by the "grandeur of this insight," for the rest of his life Freud made it the crystallization point of his thought, which could no longer tear itself away from the phenomenon of religion and the problem of humanity thereby posed. What that means, however, can only be grasped if one clarifies what Freud understood by history and how he interpreted the historical process. Here the interpretation meets with especially great difficulties, because Freud's statements on this theme are in themselves contradictory.

One thing can be maintained with certainty: at no time in his intellectual development did Freud concern himself with anything like an ahistorical metaphysics of the soul; he was interested rather in its historicity and thus in its changes.[18] For him a human being is a historical person, and Freud was occupied all his life with the problem of the time-bound nature of humankind and society, which toward the end of his life he encountered in concentrated form in the problems of religion. Likewise undisputed is the observation that the early Freud, as a representative of the Enlightenment, believed in the unilinear progress of history as a continuous upward movement.[19] Yet it is noteworthy that in place of this

unilinearity there very quickly came a certain brokenness in the
historical interpretation, which has repeatedly confused and dis-
concerted even otherwise astute interpreters of Freud. Thus Philip
Rieff ("Meaning of History and Religion," 120) correctly states that
Freud in a certain sense stands on the side of tradition in that he
reminds us of it and of its importance but that even so he attempts
something like a systematic "abortion" of tradition. Where one attempts a systematization of this opposition, as did David Riesman
("Freud and Psychoanalysis"), Freud's interpretation of history can
only be characterized as a "compromise between ambiguous and
contradictory elements." Thus it is thought that in Freud are found
both elements of the idea of progress and cyclical ideas of historical
interpretation through which he linked himself with the Greek
understanding of history. Since this second type of historical thinking dominates unequivocally in his later work, it is held that Freud
must be placed on the side of conservative thinkers. According to
the summary judgment, in Freud's view the future has no power
over the past, and for him, therefore, there is not the slightest
chance of a radical change in society; rather, in contrast to Marx,
for whom the past was always pregnant with the future, for Freud
the future is pregnant only with the past.

In response to this, however, an important objection must be
raised. Freud's interpretation of history as a constant "compulsion
to repeat," as an ever new "recurrence of the repressed," is valid
only for the pathological phenomena of neurosis. The assumption
that the human individual does not mature psychically, that in the
course of development a person encounters nothing new, is precisely characteristic of neurotic development; it may not be regarded as a general law of history. [20] If Freud—as we attempted to
show in the chapter on therapy—tried to free the patient from
precisely the vicious circle of the constant compulsion to repeat,
then that was also true for the phenomenal forms of culture: if
history exhausts itself in constant repetition, it maintains a pathological character trait, which Freud had already observed in *Totem
und Tabu*. The liberation of the human race from these compulsions
to repeat is, therefore, the real passion of his criticism of religion.

The curious interlocking of revolutionary and traditionalist traits
in Freud's later work, therefore, cannot be interpreted as a linking-up

with Greek thought, with its cyclical explanation of history; it finds its clarification rather in the observation that the aging Freud identified himself more and more strongly with a particular role, namely, that of the prophet. But Max Weber has demonstrated, in his brilliant analysis of prophetic religion, how prophecy binds together both elements. The prophet is a revolutionary and a traditionalist: "He must project the positive euphoric turn of his emotional condition into the future: as promise." Thus Freud sought to track down the history-making elements in the traditions of his own people, in the "progress in spirituality."

The Moses figure was supposed to bring him enlightenment on how it was possible in Israelite religious history to achieve such a "triumph of spirituality over sensuality," which could communicate to the Jews elation over being a chosen people, and how as a unique case in the history of human religions one could come upon the "amazing idea that a God all at once chose a people and declared them to be his people and himself to be their God." Freud's theories concerning Moses, which were presented with great discernment and considerable exegetical extravagance, can be reduced to the following fundamental ideas:

1. In the Moses tradition two sources have come together, from which two Moses figures can be reconstructed: an Egyptian Moses, who proclaimed the universal god Aton, and a Midianite Moses, who served the fire demon Yahweh, who resided on the mountain of the gods.

2. The Egyptian Moses began his hero's life by descending from the heights of his prominent position in the Egyptian court, lowering himself to the level of the children of Israel, and pledging them to the monotheism of the Aton religion, from which everything mythical, magical, and enchanted was excluded. He thereby shaped the long-term character of the Jewish people "through the rejection of magic and mysticism, stimulation toward progress in spirituality, and the summons to sublimation"; and blessed by the possession of the truth and overcome by the consciousness of being chosen, the people achieved a high estimation of the intellect and an emphasis on ethics.

3. The rebellious people killed their leader and since then have been cursed with the stigma of patricide, yet on this foundation the

religion of atonement for this monstrous crime, the substitutionary sacrifice of the son, was immediately able to develop.[21]

The soundness of Freud's theories concerning Moses with respect to exegesis and the history of religion cannot be examined here. He himself did not feel that their historical foundations were solid enough to permit publication of these works, and therefore he decided to keep them to himself. For him it was enough that he himself was able to believe in the solution to a problem that had haunted him his whole life, namely, how the existential guilt feeling of humanity had come about, on what foundation generally binding ethical demands had arisen, and which attempts at solving this problem were to be regarded as productive for the future and which ones, on the other hand, would be revealed as neurotic mechanisms. The Moses tradition thus appeared to Freud as the point where the totemistic form of religion, which can only bring constant repetitions, is transformed to the progressive steps in spirituality of a historically defined religion, which seeks to give an answer to the same problem. Thus in his old age, as once in his youth, Freud could look in amazement at that spirituality in which the concept of a "divinity encompassing the whole world" was alive, a divinity "who was no less all-loving than all-powerful, who—averse to all ceremony and magic—set as the highest goal of humanity a life in truth and justice" and summoned to joy and enjoyment. Here the interpretation of the Golgotha tragedy by Paul can be regarded as the "correct" solution to the fundamental problem of guilt. His warning applies to all forms of religious regression that allow infantile wishful thinking, do not exclude superstitious and magical elements, and thus promote the return of the repressed.

We believe, therefore, that Freudian psychoanalysis does not necessarily have to lead to the dissolution of faith itself. Rather, it can even provide critical viewpoints that could be of importance for a purification of the organized forms of the Christian faith.

6

THE CHALLENGE

Psychoanalysis as Criticism of Religion

Even if Freud himself occasionally vacillated about whether he should defiantly classify himself as "one of the worst enemies of religion" or retreat behind the religious criticism of his "great predecessors"[1] to which he merely needed to add "some psychological foundation," one thing cannot be disputed: he sought throughout his life to assume an "attitude of total rejection toward religion in any form or fashion." And if he professed that he saw it as his appointed role to contribute to the "dissolution of conventional cultural certainties" and that he had devoted a large part of his lifework to "destroying his own and humanity's illusions," then he apparently meant it precisely in this sense of his professed lack of religion. Thus for Freud there is throughout a certain pathos of appointment and mission. It was not the hubris of his own high-handedness that caused him to become a critic of religion but his obligation in regard to what he could designate mythically as Ananke or what he demythologized as the "reality outside us." "It would be wanton to let one's own caprice step into the gap and, according to personal judgment, declare this or that piece of the religious system to be more or less acceptable. These questions are too meaningful for that—one would even like to say holy." He struggled against religion not because he was rebelling against it but because in the forms in which he had come to know it, religion was not able to accomplish what it was actually there for.

Again and again, Freud saw religion under the three headings of *demand, instruction,* and *solace.* What made it the great enemy that he had to fight was that it obviously could not complete these tasks without reducing the value of life, madly distorting the picture of the real world, and violently intimidating the intelligence.[2] Against this Freud set his own "confession of faith": "We believe that it is possible for scientific endeavor to learn something about the reality of the world, through which we can increase our power and by which we can organize our life." At the same time he could only express the hope that this faith might not one day prove to be just as illusory as that of religion! Thus Freud fully recognized that a person needs something by which to organize his life, a reality outside himself that is so dependable that it can give him solace. We will have to test whether the critical probe that Freud applied to the phenomenon of religion understands how to take from the Christian faith every justification for existence, or whether it picks up only distorted images. Freud's comparison of religion with compulsive neurosis sent such a shock wave through the theological camp that it was largely overlooked that Freud had indeed identified compulsive neurosis only as the "distorted image" of religion, just as he had identified hysteria as the distorted image of art and paranoia as the distorted image of philosophy. In reality, it could be that Freud's criticism helped to liberate the faith from the distortions of its pathological doppelgänger.

AGAINST THE OBEDIENCE TABOO

At first glance it strikes one as simply absurd that Freud and his life's work are so stubbornly and repeatedly made responsible for moral decline and ethical ruin. His lifestyle and his conduct of life are those of a bourgeois moralist of prominence, and nowhere in his biography can one discover even the slightest deviation from the path of virtue. His moral judgment always remained the same whether it was a question of the "shameless Parisians" whom he had met in his youth or the friend of his fiancée who, to his horror, was living with a man she had not yet married and with whom, therefore, Freud could of course no longer associate; whether it concerned patients and the question of why they always had to tell "these most horrible, perverse details" of their sex lives, or the conviction of his old age that his dear fellow human beings—with few exceptions—were riffraff.[3] Also, in regard to psychoanalytical theories, Freud characterized as an "evil misunderstanding justified only by ignorance" the assertion that psychoanalysis expects the healing of neurotic ailments from the "free exercise of sexuality." Indeed, psychoanalysis has never spoken of giving free reign to instincts injurious to the public but, on the contrary, has given warnings and admonitions. Freud always burdened the analyst with the whole weight of moral responsibility, and without hesitation he risked his friendship with Sandor Ferenczi when he learned that Ferenczi exchanged signs of affection with his woman patients.[4] If psychoanalysis makes the recommendation that the austerity of instinct repression be relaxed, it is, naturally, only in order to allow more room for truthfulness.[5]

Now, if Freud stood in harmony with the conceptions of morality of his time both in conduct and teaching, how was it possible that he was repeatedly accused of immorality? Could it be a case here of willful and malicious misunderstanding? By no means! Basically, those who raised objection to psychoanalysis in the name of traditional morality were completely right: Freud's protest against traditional ethics was not directed simply against its material content. At this point he was even of the opinion that a new morality would have to require nothing different from the old. For him it was not at all a question of a simple inversion of the old morality, so that suddenly everything would be allowed that was previously forbidden. Freud initiated his criticism at a much deeper level: for him it was a matter of questioning the moral principle itself as it had taken shape in the schema of instruction and obedience.

Now with this, of course, Freud attacked the "greatest treasures of civilization." Indeed, he did not shy from comparing Kant's categorical imperative to the taboo precepts of primitives. Just as taboos are without any substantiation, are of unknown origin, are incomprehensible to outsiders but a matter of course to those who live under their dominion, so the categorical imperative, in its psychological nature, represents nothing different, because its purpose is "to work by compulsion and exclude any conscious motivation." Freud was not interested in the question of whether one in certain situations should behave thus or thus; he was challenged, rather, to reflect on the problem of obedience to untested authority, which he clearly recognized as a specifically German problem.[6]

Freud could see the problem of ethical decision only in its historical context. Without doubt, obedience is compelled first of all through an external authority. A great change occurs, however, as soon as this authority is internalized through the establishment of a superego. Then whenever a person is still forced to react according to precepts that are not an expression of his instinctive inclination, he lives, psychologically speaking, beyond his means and objectively must be termed a hypocrite. According to Freud's observations, however, the developmental stages of the past have by no means disappeared without a trace; rather, they remain preserved in the unconscious areas of the psyche: succession is also conditioned by coexistence. This means that every developmental stage is constantly threatened by reversion to modes of behavior that have in actuality already been outgrown. That seems, however, to have been exactly what Freud observed in the ethical behavior of the world around him and what disturbed him most deeply: the process of the "internalization" of authority seemed to be failing; it did not lead to the situation in which one could actually enter the realm of freedom that humanity had created for itself vis-à-vis nature and the tutelage of religion and tradition. When external courts of punishment are lacking, human beings punish themselves. Gods that in external reality have been deposed return again as terrifying demons in the interior of the soul and assume their dominion there. The withdrawal of the binding power of religion is purchased with an increase in neuroses. This process shows that humanity is not only much more immoral than it believes but also much more moral than it realizes: one sees people become ill just as often when they try to shed an ideal as when they want to achieve it.

Above all, the phenomena of "moral masochism" made it impossible for Freud to acknowledge the taboo character of conscience. After Kant formulated the categorical imperative, the conscience was repeatedly seen as something like a voice of God, and even Heidegger turned conscience into a holy realm, not to be questioned, from which one is called "in the manner of silence." Thus today's thinking also runs the risk of turning the conscience into an oasis of transcendence in the midst of the historical existence of humanity. In contrast to this, Freud undertook something like a critical destruction of the conscience as a transcendent absolute in that he succeeded in taking the explanation of the phenomenon of conscience in its historical determination and development a good bit further than seemed possible or advisable before him.

Just as anxiety points to the fundamental human reality of having to possess objects, so conscience rests on the other fundamental reality of the possibility of human relationship, namely, identification. It is closely related to the prehistory of the Oedipus complex, that emotional attitude of the little boy, which is easily verified through observation: he would like to possess his mother and thus be like his father. With the little girl the opposite situation comes about. In the childhood play of this phase of development, the imitation of the parent of the same sex becomes more and more prominent, so that this parent is, so to speak, taken up into the child's own person. The ego of the boy is "changed according to the model of the father." Through the assumption of the parental ideal into one's own personality, the Oedipus complex is gradually resolved. Into its place steps the superego, which represents the remnants of relinquished object possessions and which is given a special position in the ego. For Freud this superego is the "representation of all moral limitations, the advocate of aspiration to perfection, in short, that which has become psychologically available to us from the so-called higher things in human life." Through the process of instinct separation, it can assume aggressive tendencies into itself, and the erotic component no longer has the power to bind the powers of destruction. Freud could easily observe, "The more a person masters his aggression, the greater becomes his superego's inclination toward aggression against his ego." It can take on outright cruel, sadistic traits. Concerning those who, vis-à-vis psychoanalysis, had brought to expression their "trembling apprehension over the continuation of the higher things in the human being," Freud could now point to the superego. It had

> in consequence of its formation history the most extensive connection with the phylogenic acquisition, the archaic heritage of the individual. What belongs to the most profound in the individual spiritual life becomes, through ideal formation, the highest in the human soul

according to our evaluations. . . . Commandments and prohibitions have remained powerful in the ideal ego and now as conscience exercise moral censorship. The tension between the claims of conscience and the achievements of the ego are perceived as a feeling of guilt.

Thus are the phenomena of conscience incorporated into the historicity of human existence. They are the historical remnants of historical forces, that is, the educating powers with which the developing person identified. An original, so to speak, natural ability to distinguish good and evil is rejected; the actual moving force of conscience is the originally dominating "anxiety over the loss of love." It sets something like an avalanche into motion:

In the beginning, of course, the conscience (more correctly, the anxiety that later becomes the conscience) is the cause of instinct rejection, but later the relationship is reversed. Every instinct rejection now becomes a dynamic source of conscience; every new rejection increases its strictness and intolerance; and if we could only bring it into better harmony with the history of the origin of conscience that is known to us, we would be tempted to profess the paradoxical statement that conscience is the result of instinct rejection, or the rejection of instinct (imposed upon us from outside) creates conscience, which then demands further instinct rejection.[7]

The discovery that strictness of the superego comes about even with more lenient upbringing made it necessary for Freud finally to resort to the "phylogenetic model" of the father in the primal horde and to anchor his theory in the ambivalent feelings of the sons toward the father:

The sons hated him, but they also loved him; after the hate was satisfied through aggression, love came into prominence in repentance for the deed, established the superego through identification with the father, gave it the power of the father as if for punishment for the aggressive deed perpetrated against him, and created the restrictions that were to guard against a repetition of the deed.

Thus, for Freud, conscience is the expression of the ambiguity of the eternal struggle between eros and the instinct toward destruction and death. As Paul Ricoeur shows, at this very point there would have been an opportunity to press forward to a deepened understanding of the religion of the son. The turning point of the whole drama of patricide is the "point in time when the brothers reach an agreement not to renew the patricide among themselves."

This is highly significant, for by forbidding fratricide, this agreement creates a history and thus the possibilities of an ordered social togetherness. Yet Freud was so occupied with the symbolic repetition of the murder in the totem feast that, without any consideration of historical recognition in the figure of the son, he could only see the figure of a murderer—the ringleader of the revolt. That the destiny of faith could be allied with this fraternal union rather than with the constant renewal of the patricide and thus that the religion of the son could be a genuine forward step beyond the father complex—this perception escaped Freud, although with his teaching on the conscience he had struck at the heart of any form of pure obedience to the superego as an ethical principle and delivered it up to ambiguity.

Yet what would Freud offer instead? In moral masochism, he was confronted with a regression, a step backward: morality was again sexualized, the Oedipus complex revived; progress, on the other hand, would consist in an overcoming and desexualization of the Oedipus complex and in the superego's becoming "sufficiently impersonal." This open objectivity of the phenomenon of conscience, however, can only be achieved if it has lost its taboo character, which means that the rejection of certain stirrings of desire need rely on nothing else but rather is sure of itself.[8] In contrast to this, Freud demanded that ethical decision be based on insight.

For Freud this meant, in the first place, that ethical demands, which religion also wants to emphasize, require another, nonreligious foundation. He had given very serious thought to the question of just what would become of public morality if the religious obligation on which this morality had been based for centuries could no longer claim general validity. For him it was too great a risk to make ethical requirements, which are essential to human society, dependent on belief in God. In this connection, two things are noteworthy:

1. Never for a moment did Freud doubt that ethical requirements that came about rationally through the primacy of the intellect would set, with respect to content, the same goals as those aspired to by the faithful in the name of God, and thus that the rivalry was only temporary and not irreconcilable, since ultimately both hoped for the same thing. Freud wasted no thought, however, on the

question of why this must be so. Perhaps it would then have occurred to him that his criticism of religion did not strike at the heart
of faith but rather made visible, behind the "religious phenomenon," something that even he could not escape.

2. Also remarkable was the "rational foundation" of the ethical
commandment against the background of the basic Freudian perception that in the conflict between intellectual and emotional motivation, the former always comes off second-best. Certainly there
had been a time in Freud's development when he could place "no
authority above reason." But the confidence that with time reason
would gain dominance in the life of the human soul still remained a
hope for the future, a utopia that lay far off in the distance. He went
through a phase of deep resignation and skepticism in which he
held that one could not imagine how bad the instability and the
addiction to authority of people were, and in which even the idea
of a therapeutic application of insight left him at a loss; for what
good is the truest analysis of the social neurosis, "since no one has
the authority to force therapy on the masses"?

We believe, nevertheless, that this resigned question was not
Freud's last word on the ethical problem. At least three areas are to
be sketched that indicate directions in which continuing possibilities of solution may lie. We will designate them with the key words
"freedom," "sublimation," and "love."

1. For the therapeutic situation, Freud had thought completely
through, in regard to principle and method, the question of just
what it actually means if the goal of analysis consists in creating for
the ego of the patient the freedom to decide this way or that.
It means that one must bravely resist the temptation vis-à-vis
the patient to play the role of prophet, soul-rescuer, savior. It is the
decisive rejection of an attitude that takes the patient—who is
seeking help and places himself in the hands of the therapist—and
"turns him into chattel, shapes his fate for him, seeks to force on
him our ideals and, with the pride of the creator, to shape him in
our own image, with which we are well pleased." Therefore, psychoanalysis is not supposed to place itself in the service of a particular ideology that it then forces on the patient for the purpose of
refinement. Also it cannot unburden the patient through adoption
into a society shaped in a particular way; it is rather a matter of

enrichment from within the patient himself by delivering to the ego those energies that were kept unfruitful through repression. Could the role that Freud intended for the analyst in this process not become a model for all of those who as educators, advisers, counselors, and pastors have to give guidance toward ethical decision? Then they would understand themselves only as a "catalytic agent" and trust the situation itself to reveal its possibilities for resolution, which had occurred to neither of the two partners at the beginning of the dialogue relationship. Dialogue would thus become the source of ethical decision, and ethics itself would be stripped of its compelling, enslaving, taboo character and be freed instead to become a "kind of traffic code for interaction with other people."

2. With great acuity Freud perceived that in reality there can be no eradication of evil at all. People do not want to eradicate their complexes but want rather to come to terms with them. Absolute rejection is psychologically impossible; the desire for satisfaction can only be diverted and directed toward other goals. Freud called that sublimation. In the case of sexuality, this means "exchanging [an] immediate goal for other, perhaps more highly valued and nonsexual goals." External force or the pure demand of society for good behavior appeared meaningless to Freud so long as one did not concern oneself with the "instinctual foundation." This seemed urgently necessary, above all in regard to the aggressive inclination of humanity. Even this cannot be fully eliminated but can only be "redirected." The instinct for destruction must be redirected above all by the likes of us so that we will finally stop hating because of small differences and killing for the sake of small gains. As important means to the sublimation of the aggressive instinct Freud named the desire for knowledge and the instinct for research. He especially felt, however, that it was necessary to transform selfish instincts into social ones "through the addition of erotic components."[9] But that means "appealing to the opponent, to eros," and promoting everything that produces emotional ties between people.

3. The skeptical question whether eros or the forces of aggression will be victorious, with which Freud closes his *Unbehagen in der Kultur* (Civilization and its discontents), gives to the present day the quality of a time of decision, a kairos. If a history-determining

force can be seen from the viewpoint of the return of the repressed, a decisive question will be, From which circumstances of the past and of tradition has humankind alienated itself through repression, so that it must suffer their recurrence in the bursting forth of violent conflict situations? In his later years, therefore, Freud devoted himself resolutely to researching his own tradition in the hope that through conscious interaction with the past he might also better master the future. In this, to be sure, his historical-philosophical view was focused on one leitmotif, that of patricide. With a certain monomania he tried on his own to resolve the "magnificence of the world's interrelatedness," which repeatedly led him to humility. In the process he committed the same "outrage against the magnificent diversity of human life" for which he faulted others. Inwardly, the bit of knowledge that he found in this way forced him to answer very unambiguously with his personal life the question that was posed by the ambiguity of human existence between libido and destrudo. In his discussion of reality, which necessitated the reality principle, he could see various possibilities. One can defend oneself through some kind of alienation but thereby fall into isolation and loneliness. One can also turn to an assault on nature and devote oneself to the illusion of working for the happiness of all, until one realizes that humankind is still not becoming happier. One can also devote oneself to art as a source of pleasure and solace in life. "Yet the mild anesthesia under which art places us provides no more than a fleeting escape from the cares of life and is not strong enough to make one forget real misery." Only a "technology of the art of living" seemed to Freud suited to solving these problems:

> It would also not be satisfied with the almost wearily acquiescing goal of aversion avoidance; rather, it passes that goal indifferently by and holds fast to the original passionate striving for the positive realization of happiness. Perhaps it really comes closer to this goal than any other method. I mean, naturally, that direction of life that takes love as its center and expects all satisfaction to come from loving and being loved.

Freud held this "technology of life based on the happiness value of love" to be so significant that he felt he had much more still to say about it, and indeed the topic was never to disappear from his publications and statements. His letters reveal a personality that is thoroughly permeated with love. So to Oskar Pfister he wrote, "I have, as you grant, done a lot for love." Vis-à-vis the Freud of the scientific objectivity of proceedings, there stood in his letters a person who simply did not have the heart to send away patients with seemingly no prospect. And a case history could also be reported in this very human form: "I began to feel sorry for the poor boy, . . . was close to giving up on him again, but there is something touching about him that holds me back. . . . His unbearableness has been happily overcome; I have taken a direct fancy to him." Freud turned his attention emphatically against the misunderstanding of the basic position of analysis as a pure mirror function, because this "spoils the effectiveness of analysis through a certain sullen indifference," but his boundless respect for the individuality of the patient never permitted him to lose sight of one thing: "However warmheartedly the analyst may conduct himself, he can still not take it upon himself to replace God and providence for the analysand."

Freud's desire to bring humankind help in living was possible for him only in love and through love. Often one gets the direct impression that it was painful for him to profess love, because that could place him under the suspicion of sentimentality and enthusiasm. Thus he made the adventurous attempt to substantiate love from the standpoint of expediency: "I myself held on to love . . . because I had to declare it just as indispensable as technology for the maintenance of the human species." But also: "Truth is only the absolute goal of science, while love is a completely independent goal of life." Freud was able to understand and accommodate his whole lifework under the one caption "healing through love." With this attitude he endured even his long spiritual and severe bodily sufferings, took upon himself persecution and disdain, and kept his irrepressible humor into old age. He considered it his great mission to work for the maintenance of peace in a way that would promote everything "that produces emotional ties between people." The whole of civilization "is a process in service to eros, which intends to unite separated human individuals into a great oneness, into humankind." Just as the doctor in the analytical "work of education" avails himself of a component of love in order to bring about the patient's progress from the pleasure principle to the reality principle, so Freud wanted to open up the possibilities of love to the whole society on its ethical path. The divine pair Logos and Ananke, in which he believed as a young man, was transformed in his old age into Eros and Ananke, love and reality.

Freud's leveling of the ethical problem in the historical existence of humanity was not so completely successful as his enlightened understanding might have wished. With his extremely great scientific honesty he had to admit that there was a remainder that kept him from simply dismissing the phenomena of faith as superstition, since in the unconscious of his patients he repeatedly came across structures that could not be explained on the basis of individual life history but were strikingly parallel to the tradition. All old cultural powers and their conceptual structures—those of the Middle Ages, animistic antiquity, and even the Stone Age—seemed to be still alive in humankind. It was probably this observation above all that drove Freud to ever new approaches to an ever-deeper understanding of religious doctrines.

AGAINST THE PIOUS DELUSION

The fact that Freud took the liberty of calling religious ideas a "delusion" under certain conditions seemed automatically to keep a theologian from delving further and deeper into this subject. After the catchword "delusion"—so it was widely held—any further discussion was superfluous, because faith and its manifestations were thereby subjected to the radical suspicion of being nonsense, were regarded as insanity and dismissed. This attitude, however, measures the catchword "delusion" against the concepts of the old psychiatry and completely overlooks the fact that here too Freud created a fundamental change. As delusory formations he understood meaningful reactions of the psyche that come about under certain conditions and, among other things, are marked by the following characteristics:

1. Delusion is not an illness of the psyche but rather its attempt to heal itself. Delusion comes about as a reaction to the loss or destruction of the ego's object relationships.

2. Thus the patient lives in a special world in which only the "currency of neurosis" has value; this means that the things that are operative for him are those that are intensively thought, affectively imagined; agreement with external reality is secondary.

3. Delusory formations originate through a particular linguistic peculiarity, namely, when a word concept is treated like an object concept, when a linguistic expression that we understand symbolically is taken literally, and thus the "slap in the face" or the "stab in the back" of an offending statement is perceived as a real event.

If we transfer these reflections from psychopathology into the realm of religious criticism, it means that with the catchword "delusion," Freud criticized religious statements about life that have lost contact with their actual reality and have withdrawn into a special sphere of reality in which only the "currency of religion" has value and symbols are misunderstood "literally" in that such statements attempt to take them word for word.

As he endeavored to understand these phenomena, Freud saw himself involved, so to speak, in a war on two fronts. On the one hand, he was not able to concede to the mythical formations in question here the character of reality in the scientific sense; that is, for him they were neither the products of experience nor the end results of thinking. On the other hand, however, he believed that one would commit an injustice if one were to "casually discard" the mythical material; indeed, psychoanalysis had discovered a number of areas of life that obey the same structural laws as myth yet are not at all done and gone but rather are of decisive influence on the lives of people living in the present. In addition to childhood, there are above all fairy tales and sagas, folklore and jokes, in which the suppressed mythos inevitably returns; then the broad area of mental illnesses such as neuroses and psychoses; and finally that bit of mythical experience that every "normal" person can also afford, the dream.

Since the first beginnings of research into myths, it has been known that myth represents something that we can observe in the mental life of a child. Yet myth researchers did not see themselves in a position to define this element positively and were satisfied with a negative definition as *imbecillitas*, "inability, failure." When Freud designated the mental stimulations of the childhood years as the element that made possible an understanding of mythos, he was thinking of a number of abilities still possessed by a child that are foreign to the adult because of the necessities and compulsions of his upbringing. Thus the child—for whom mature, genital sexuality is still a closed area and whose sexual interest, through partial instincts, is concentrated on, say, oral and rectal areas—can integrate these regions meaningfully into his childlike "sexual theories" by assuming impregnation through the mouth and birth as excretion. Precisely these and similar themes, however, recur in myths and fairy tales, so that Freud saw in them a key to understanding. Infantile theories of sex are certainly false biologically, but they contain existential truth to the extent that the interest of the child is directed toward the regions of the body that he uses. The world is interpreted as a context of meaning in correspondence with this affective participation in phylogenetically foreordained developmental laws. In countless sagas and myths Freud sees even the question of the anatomical difference between the sexes treated, which plainly causes an "uproar in the child's emotional life."

Psychoanalytic researchers into myth were repeatedly and extremely amazed by the fact that the old world accorded to sexual organs and functions what to our minds is quite an enormous importance, and it finally brought Freud to the idea that an especially intimate connection must exist between symbol and sexuality. Thus he even occupied himself with the bizarre linguistic theory of one H. Sperber (Uppsala), who wanted to trace the origin of language and symbol back to the idea that every word once had two meanings, of which one must have designated sexual, the other everyday activities. As questionable and ultimately untenable as this theory appears today, so important, on the other hand, are the parallels between the linguistic habits of myth and of children subsequently discovered by Freud. Indeed, for the child, just as for myth, language is so very real that he can treat words like objects, and for him a consonance in names also means a correspondence in reality. Indeed, in the child, conscious and unconscious things still lie undistinguished side by side, and it is the work of the linguistic function to enable even internal processes in the ego to acquire the quality of consciousness.

Freud came across the parallel between neurosis and the mythical way of thinking very early in his studies on hysteria. Here he especially noticed the significance of language in the illness. Indeed, it is a full-fledged surrogate for action. Freud could even speak of an "organ language," of the strange fact that in individual analysis sessions, symptoms such as certain organic pains began "to join in the discussion" and caused complaints "until the pain was talked away." Freud believed that hysteria, by circumventing external tradition, had at its disposal immediate access to a distant past. "Perhaps it is not right to say that hysteria creates such situations through symbolization; perhaps it did not take linguistic usage as a model at all but rather drew with it from a common source." Later Freud coined for this common source the expression "the archaic heritage of humanity" and decided to regard the unconscious in general as the "collective, common possession of humankind," since the psychic remnants of mythical antiquity had become the legacy that "in every new generation needed only development, not acquisition." Thus there is an "innate symbolism" that comes from the time of language development and is familiar to all children without receiving any instruction. Freud owed the deepest insight into such an assumed "basic language" to the striking similarity of the neurotic symptoms and utterances of patients to the modes of expression of the mythical tradition. It inspired a whole group of researchers to special efforts in this area and even moved them to initiate their own journal, *Imago*. Even with the linguistic expressions of schizophrenics, however, there appeared again and again the "trait of hypochondria," which caused these utterances to become organ language. In this, the condensation and displacement could go so far "that a single word, suited thereto through manifold relationships, takes over the representation of a whole train of thought." Except in the mythical-symbolical way of speaking, Freud had been able to observe this so-called "primary process" only in dreams.

The dream is just as needful of interpretation as is mythos, but both of them are subjected by the "scientific age" to the same suspicion of being nonsense. Freud was the first to develop the hermeneutical principle that in mental life there can be nothing that is absolutely meaningless. Thus he approached the dream in a way no different from an old, now unintelligible text: "In fact, the interpretation of a dream is fully analogous to the deciphering of an old picture language such as Egyptian hieroglyphics." The interpretations of psychoanalysis are nothing more than "translations from a mode of expression foreign to us into one familiar to our thinking."

Behind the "language of the dream," the manifest dream content, one must find the "latent dream idea." It is thereby revealed that the dream "belongs to a highly archaic system of expression." Freud saw this archaic element of dream language in the fact that its concepts are still ambivalent, that in them opposing meanings are still united, and that, above all, it is completely realized and conveyed by symbols, that is, by "substitutions and comparisons on the basis of similarities," in which to a large extent "the point of comparison has escaped our conscious knowledge"; therefore it must "come from the earliest stages of language development and concept formation." Just like the language of myth, dream language is the mode of expression of unconscious mental activity, which, to be sure, speaks several dialects and therefore presents certain difficulties to interpretation.

The point of departure for Freud's attempt to achieve an interpretation of myths was the consideration that in the history of humankind there must be a reciprocal effect between human nature, cultural development, and the remnants of primeval experiences that is just as strong as the dynamic conflicts within the individual between ego, id, and superego. Thus, the former can be regarded as a reflection of the latter "repeated on a broad stage." Consequently, Freud could not regard mythos as "primitive science," for the first impetus toward myth formation did not come from a theoretical need for an explanation of natural phenomena but rather from the same complexes that psychoanalysis had found on the basis of dreams and symptom formations. It was Freud's opinion that all previous attempts at the explanation of myths turned out to be so unsatisfactory because they suffered from a "psychological provisionality"; that is, it is hard to get at myths with a pure psychology of consciousness. Only depth psychology can consider itself to be the legitimate successor of mythology. Thus it seems possible to take the findings gained from dreams and from psychoanalytic therapy and apply them to the products of myth. Myths and fairy tales can be interpreted in the same way as dreams and symptoms. That means, methodologically, that a fundamental distinction must be made between the manifest formations of the mythos, which were shaped through systematic distortion in the course of myth development, and its latent, original forms. In the interpretation, however, the process of distortion must be reversed. Yet without consideration of our perceiving mental apparatus, this would be an abstraction without practical interest. Freud was of the opinion "that every person possesses in his unconscious mental activity an apparatus that allows him to interpret the reactions of other people, that is, to reverse the distortions that the other person has added to the expression of his emotional stirrings." Myths and things in the unconscious are thus linked together in a circle: if it was possible earlier to interpret childhood memories with the help of mythic themes, then one could now understand myths better with the help of the mental life of a child, for one can still demonstrate in the child's psychic life today the same archaic elements that in primeval times once ruled human culture in general.

Yet what should be the actual focus of the interpretation? What is hiding behind the mythic distortions and misrepresentations? It was not at all Freud's opinion that with interpretation the mythic conception would dissolve into nothing. As little as he could see truth in myths in the scientific sense—that is, empirical findings and the results of reason—he tried very hard to find in them a form of truth, because he saw at work in them "motifs that are still effective today." He had scarcely coined his formula of religion as illusion when he was already dissatisfied with it. For Freud, what was decisive about the formula of the historical truth of religion was that it contained something that must be regarded "as the return of long-forgotten, significant processes in primal history." From that, it followed "that the human race has a prehistory, and since it is unknown, that is, forgotten, such a conclusion almost has the weight of a postulate." Thus the decisive statement on religion reads, "To the extent that it is distorted, one may term it *delusion;* to the extent that it brings a return of the past, one must call it *truth.*"

What does this mean? Involved in the process of myth formation is an unconscious mechanism that causes the mythic tradition to become a delusionary misrepresentation of reality. The symbolic character of its assertions must yield to a literalistic understanding that is valid only in a separate realm of reality. If the unconscious "missing link" can be found and interpreted with the help of one's own unconscious—that is, if distortions and misrepresentations can be reversed—then the mythos will represent reality. Freud, however, could not be satisfied with recognizing that an almost ontological structure of reality is thereby revealed. On the one hand, even he would have liked to assume that the idea of only one God had such an overpowering effect on humanity because it is a bit of eternal truth, but then his skepticism left him no peace: "No one had otherwise been able to establish that the human intellect possesses an especially good nose for the truth." And so he turned by chance in a direction that he designated with the caption "historical truth": we believe not that there is only one God today but that in primeval times there was a great person who left behind such impressions in the human soul.

Thus we stand before what is certainly one of the most vulnerable parts of the Freudian interpretation of religion: his mythos of the primal horde. As we have already seen,[10] Freud himself had sensed his weakness. He knew, naturally, that the primal-horde theory was pure speculation, and he himself called it a "just-so story." Into his old age, however, Freud was so fascinated with his idea that even in the theories concerning Moses, alongside many important insights, he still accommodated a variation of the primal horde's patricide. His stubbornness at this point has to appear all the more incomprehensible since the search for "historical truth" in individual therapy had, indeed, maneuvered Freud into a cul-de-sac in which he was inclined, in resignation similar to Breuer's, to abandon everything. It was that stage in his development in which sexual trauma seemed definitely to be the cause of neurosis, but it was impossible that sexual seduction could have occurred as a real experience with the frequency that he at first assumed. At that time Freud found a solution by granting to the inner, psychic reality the same dignity and traumatizing power as the outer reality. In his interpretation of religion, however, he could not decide to take the same step.

Of course, he asked himself whether the "creative consciousness of guilt," which had still not been extinguished among us, could not just as well be a reaction to sheer impulses of hostility against the father, since neurosis is indeed characterized by the fact that it places the psychic reality above the factual. Yet he did not pursue the discussion of this question to the end but instead broke it off impatiently.

At this point Freud set out on a path on which we can no longer follow him. Nonetheless, the search for the "historical truth" netted Freud some viewpoints that can serve as criteria for the historical character of faith.

AGAINST INFANTILE WISHFUL
THINKING AS SOLACE

In his search for the historical truth of religion, it occurred to Freud almost as a "byproduct" of his research that among religious manifestations there were two completely different structures. The one always seemed, in ever new repetitions, to reach back to the old and to renew it; the other was directed toward the future, brought about progress and sublimations, and in short established a history.

Freud regarded totemic religion as the prototype of the first kind, the ahistorical-regressive structure. Here the guilty conscience of the sons who slew the father does not become something creative, something historically powerful; rather, in the compulsion of an always-repeated cycle, it can only make it a duty "to repeat over and over again the crime of patricide in the sacrifice of the totemic animal." Wherever Freud came upon such elements of the "compulsion to repeat" in the form of religious manifestations, he presumed that the same mechanism was at work as in the formation of compulsive symptoms in neurosis: the actual context of meaning is lost, forgotten, repressed, unconscious, and now the history-forming powers are blocked; everything remains in the same place and always turns around the same axis. The future cannot happen, because the past retains its power and repeatedly blocks the way. In many respects Freud was also able to uncover such regressive traits in Christianity. Thus, for example, when Holy Communion is seen as nothing more than a repetition, it comes precariously close to a totemic meal and is itself nothing but a new removal of the father, a repetition of the atoning deed. Also, vis-à-vis Judaism, certain formulations of the Christian faith could be designated as regression to the extent that they open themselves to the invasion of superstitious, magical, and mystical elements instead of constantly cleansing themselves of these heathen elements.

Responsible for this tendency toward an ahistorical quality, in Freud's view, was the unchangeability of the repressed, the curious fact that the category of time seemed to have no validity in the unconscious.[11] Therefore, the more things are passed on unconsciously in a tradition—that is, not on the basis of communication but immediately in the structures of the id—the more compulsive and unchangeable will be this tradition. It will then develop a nonverbal, anti-enlightened affect and seek to assure its preservation by conveying religious doctrines to the children at an age when they have neither the interest in them nor the ability to comprehend their significance. In Freud's opinion, there is, next to the sexual, yet another, religious, restraint placed on thinking, and its effect is especially fateful because we have no means besides our intelligence to master our instinctual nature.

In the Freudian representation of religious phenomena, however, there are also traits that have a decided history-establishing power. Basically, it is the "transformation of the patriarchal horde into a fraternal community" that already carries the structure, but Freud gave it no further attention. Not until the Moses figure did he see these traits clearly. The idea that Moses climbed down from his high position and descended to the children of Israel had an enormous history-shaping power. That is to say, this event established the concept that—as the only case in the history of religion—God initiated a history with a people. The concomitant faith in a God that one cannot see "means a setting-aside of sensory perception in favor of an abstract idea, the triumph of the intellect over the senses, a rejection of instinct." In Christianity as well, Freud could see events that open the future and thus establish history: for example, that Christ went and sacrificed his own life and thus redeemed the fraternal multitude from original sin; or the fact that Christ's relationship to each individual in the mass of believers was that of a benevolent older brother, and that before him all are alike and therefore a "democratic impulse" could go out through the church and from the church.

We must stop here, although the examples could be multiplied. Freud himself probably did not realize that with the distinction between an ahistorical compulsion to repeat and a history-establishing liberation from the past for the future, he had designated one, if not *the*, decisive characteristic of the Judeo-Christian tradition of biblical thinking. For him it was at first nothing but the open objectivity of a result found in the field of therapy. He made, of course, the issue of regression or progression the central instrument of his criticism of religion. In closing, we would like to illustrate this with a few more examples.

Freud's best-known interpretation of religion, which also includes his sharpest criticism, starts with the equation of the religious phase with the childhood phase of the human race. Just as in individual development childhood is dominated by the pleasure principle, that is, by being entangled in wishes, so the religious phase is marked by the strength of its "infantile" wishes. Yet Freud is extremely distrustful of the power of human wishful stirrings and thus of the temptations of the pleasure principle. The doctrines of religion seemed to him to represent the very "fulfillment of the oldest, strongest, most urgent wishes of humanity." Freud called this wishful character illusion. At this point, to be sure, we must remember that in Freud's opinion the logical opposite of illusion was not error but reality. An illusion, however, does not necessarily have to be in contradiction with reality; many illusions can even be changed into reality. But as the inner structure of reality is the test of reality, so the wish is the test of illusion. Yet for Freud, since his early days, all physical life actually sprang out of the opposition between reality and wish fulfillment. Therefore, under no circumstances could he let this tense opposition be destroyed. Happiness, for him, was the belated fulfillment of a prehistoric wish, and religion seemed again and again to be harnessed in service of the search for happiness.

Yet humankind cannot remain forever a child; the world is no nursery. "Education to reality" becomes humanity's most important and most timely task. In keeping with this education to reality are neither euphonious humanitarian phrases nor the insincerities and intellectual bad manners with which the philosophers replace God "with an impersonal, shadowy, abstract principle." Freud wanted to hold before them the admonition "You shall not take the name of the Lord in vain."

In contrast to that, Freud saw reality represented in an attitude that he could express in this way:

> When we have begun to get a feeling for the magnificence of the world's interrelatedness and its necessities, we easily lose our own

144

little ego. Lost in wonder and having become truly humble, we forget too easily that we ourselves are a part of those working forces and that we may try, according to the extent of our personal strength, to change a little bit of that necessary course of the world—a world in which the small is still no less marvelous and significant than the great.

Freud lived according to the reality principle in that he made sacrifices not only to the god Logos, who later became Eros, but also to the god Ananke, to unrelenting reality. In order to stand firm with reality, of course, one must be freed from all wishful thinking.

It seemed beyond Freud's comprehension that all of this could lie within the realm of faith. He observed laconically that if the believer was ready to subject himself to the unsearchable ways of God, he could actually spare himself the detour through religion. Here too we must assert that a dimension and possibility of faith passed Freud by simply because he was not familiar with it and did not believe it possible.

We would like to leave as an open question whether Freud, in his lifelong occupation with the religious phenomenon, was basically searching for a solution to his own problem, that is, for a mature form of faith that would correspond to the state of psychic maturity for which he strived with his patients. It would have had to be a form of faith that had progressed from the lack of freedom in taboo obedience to the freedom of responsibility through insight, a faith that did not distort reality through delusion and which above all did not remain bound to an ahistorical metaphysics of the soul but that, presuming for itself no right to dogmatic rigidity, would be ready with Freud "repeatedly to plow up the vineyard." That the inner dynamic of such historical existence is not comfortable wishful thinking was expressed by Freud with a word that we want to place at the close of our reflections, a word that can serve as his uncomfortable confession of faith and life and that he illustrated in a tragic way with his own life, yet that also contains a bit of the solace that was so characteristic of Freud: "As long as a person suffers, he can still accomplish something."

NOTES

1. PRELIMINARY QUESTIONS: FREUD IN THE MIRROR OF THEOLOGICAL LITERATURE

1. Pfister incorporated psychoanalysis into his system of "critical transcendental realism," which he had elaborated almost ten years earlier and in which he had adopted a position of psychophysical parallelism.

2. "I would turn my back on theology at any time if it obligated me to a naive faith in authority or intended to force me to give up scientific methods."

3. [*Entwirklichung der Realität, Erinnerungsverluste,* and *Überwirklichung.*]

4. This, incidentally, brought him Freud's biting reproach of insincerity, since Freud could not understand at all how Pfister could get himself involved so intensively in such "muck" (Freud and Pfister, *Psychoanalysis and Faith*).

5. Pfister's investigation of love before marriage culminated in the thesis—which has not lost any of its relevance even today—that the problems of love originate from the fact "that the moral demands on love have increased immensely over the course of a long cultural development without gaining the psychological means to satisfy those refined needs for love through understanding and effective achievement." On the intertwining of epistemological problems with the problem of love ("One must first grasp the epistemological conditions of the subject before one is capable of appreciating the nature of love in general and in particular cases"), he anticipated ideas that did not find broader circulation until Jean-Paul Sartre (who said, "The problem of language is parallel to that of love").

6. In this, Pfister did not overlook at all the fact that such an analytical pastoral care could work only in a corrective and preparatory way; he contrasted it as "synthetic pastoral care" with actual proclamation, which for him, of course, had to follow.

7. It seems to have escaped Pfister that he violated here his own principle according to which, even in the field of religion, "disregarded reality tends to bring itself to bear with overwhelming power."

8. "Just as Freud healed the compulsive neurotic through his regaining love and realizing it appropriately, so also Jesus. He taught people to love and thereby destroyed religious compulsive neurosis."

9. Thus Pfister wrote to Freud, "I cannot have a good discussion with you about religion, because you completely reject philosophy" (Freud and Pfister, *Psychoanalysis and Faith*).

10. "Whoever lives for the truth, lives in God; and whoever strives for the liberation of love, remains in God, according to John 4:16. If you were to lift up into consciousness and experience there your integration into the great relationships, then I would even like to say of you, 'A better Christian never lived!'" (ibid.).

11. In the beginning he labeled Freud's "ideological background" materialistic; later, agnostic.

12. Apparently the theologians were impressed with Maag's statements that the truest and most successful teachings about the soul would always be those of Christianity, and that the great reality of the soul was still God.

13. E. Pfennigsdorf. The argument comes originally from Ernst Jahn.

14. Thus Horst Fichtner. He summarily asserted that the only effective force in psychoanalysis was suggestion—absolutely forbidden by Freud—and that the psychoanalyst aspired to the superego position. But in the same breath, he faulted psychoanalysis for offering only friendly understanding instead of encouragement and strengthening of the will, and for thus wiping away the concepts of sin and guilt. Moreover, the concept of the unconscious or subconscious is immoral!

15. In another pastoral-care text expressly oriented toward depth psychology, Walter Uhsadel believes that he can afford to draw a completely misunderstood and distorted picture of the Freudian teaching of the ego as well as repression and sublimation.

16. Hans Asmussen. The same argument is taken up later by Helmut Thielicke, who under the influence of a novel by Gertrud von Le Fort speaks of the "dreadful peace" of the psychoanalyst.

17. Georg Wobbermin. Wilfried Daim also tried to construct something like an "ideological core" of Freudian teachings, to which he could concede no future.

18. Likewise, Otto Haendler held Freud out as a "classical example of the amalgamation of ideological prejudice."

19. The same attitude stands in the background when essential statements are traced back to the "spirit of the times" and therefore rejected, or when it is maintained that Freud has "delivered the deathblow to all suprapsychological spiritualities such as morality, justice, and art."

20. To be sure, Uhsadel draws from this the exact opposite conclusion

from the one we would like to draw and holds it to be all the more unfruitful to have an encounter between theology and psychoanalysis.

21. Cf. Tillich, *The Courage to Be*, where Freud's death-wish theory is related to the *libido moriendi* of Seneca. Tillich presents the overcoming of the pleasure principle in both.

22. It is also noteworthy that where he criticizes Freud, Tillich does it with argumentation that is exactly opposite that of theology before him. This becomes clear especially in his critique of the libido concept, which he calls puritanical because with Freud it is seen only under the torment of never-achieved satisfaction and thus only reflects the human condition of existential alienation; in its essential aspect, however, libido is not only concupiscence but also an element of love and thus a normal striving toward vital self-fulfillment. In my opinion, incidentally, this criticism applies only to the early Freud and not to his concept of the libido described in later years as the "longing for ever-greater unity."

23. I cannot follow Bernet in his argumentation at this point and I consider it an erroneous interpretation. Perhaps it came about because Bernet approaches Freud from a one-sided, psychosomatic standpoint, sees him largely through the glasses of Medard Boss, and relies perhaps a little too uncritically on the early works of Theodor Bovet. In that regard, however, he could also have let Bovet tell him that Freud was, indeed, not attempting to explain causally—precisely because there is nothing there to explain—but to interpret symbols, for this alone is appropriate to the nature of the spiritual. According to Bovet, however, Freud had also, already in the "theoretical superstructure" of his research into hysteria, crossed over to a historical point of view, in the sense that hysteria is regarded as the result of an understandable development and thus acquires a history. Finally, as for Bernet's criticism that in dream interpretation the dream is robbed of its concrete context and reduced to abstract symbolism, only with difficulty can I bring this into harmony with Freud's technical instructions according to which the dream may not be decoded, as if with a dictionary, but need only be taken into the hermeneutical circle by means of the prior understanding of related ideas. We will have to pursue this whole complex of issues in the context of chap. 4.

2. THE MAN: FREUD AND HIS INTELLECTUAL ROOTS

1. See Fromm, *Sigmund Freud's Mission*. The inelegant question of Freud's impotence can scarcely be answered with the clarity that Fromm would like. Also, it may well be of less importance for posterity than that of his intellectual potency, which seems quite beyond question!

2. The biographer Jones (*Life and Work*) finds this remark of Freud's incomprehensible. He believes that Freud could have meant this at best only in the ethical sense. It is interesting that Freud's remark on his Bible

readings was expunged from the later editions of his *Selbstdarstellung* (self-portrait), without its being possible to determine who was responsible for the deletion.

3. Therefore, with a certain degree of justification, Wilfried Daim points to a "blockade in Freud's thinking" that "could have come about through repressed unconscious tendencies, which, in contrast to his conscious nihilism, were in a completely different vein."

4. "I know that the reading of Goethe's beautiful essay 'Die Natur' . . . made my decision to enroll in medicine."

5. Goethe: "We should, it seems to me, always be more observant of how the things about which we want to gain knowledge differ than how they resemble one another." And Freud: "I feel very little need for synthesis. The unity of this world seems so self-evident to me that it is not worth giving it any prominence. What interests me is the separation and organization of what would otherwise flow together in a primeval mush."

6. Goethe: "Science is actually the prerogative of humanity, and if it leads a person again and again to the great concept that everything is a harmonious unit, and yet again that he is also a harmonious unit, then this great concept will remain much richer and fuller for him than if he rests in a comfortable mysticism that likes to hide its poverty in a respectable obscurity."

7. Goethe: "Just as it is good not to exclude any power of the soul from use in common life, so should each one, I think, be allowed to cooperate in the propagation of science."

8. Merlan ("Brentano and Freud") even traces Freud's dualistic conceptions to Brentano's teachings on love (*vis concupiscibilis*) and hate (*vis irascibilis*).

9. Especially on the issue of the emancipation of women Freud criticizes Mill very sharply. In regard to him, Freud adopts a downright hair-raising reactionary position, which he defends at length in letters to his fiancée.

10. "Men already abstracted and generalized before Plato wrote, or they would not have been human beings; but they did so by an unconscious working of the laws of association, which resembled an instinct" (Mill, "Grote's Plato," 421).

11. ". . . that knowledge is 'to be evolved out of the mind itself, not poured into it from without'" (ibid., 423, citing Grote).

12. This attitude is scarcely to be traced back, as by Igor Caruso, to the fact that Freud was only a "mediocre philosopher," but is rather to be attributed, as by Ernst von Aster, to Freud's "deep mistrust of any form of idealistic metaphysics."

13. "Consciousness, whatever it may be, does not come to every activity of the cerebral cortex, and not to the individual activity every time in the same degree; it is not something that is bound to one locality in the nervous system."

NOTES

14. Bernheim. On this point Freud was soon to think quite differently.

15. "Even mature men, who through later personal experience have liberated their brains from those influences, in spite of all of their mental independence and freethinking, preserve inside them a number of old conceptions from which they can never free themselves" (Bernheim).

16. "There are, just for the human spirit, ideas that are accepted through imitation . . . and are passed down like instincts from one generation to another. . . . It is impossible to destroy them through rational means, and dangerous to intend to do so by force" (Liébault).

17. A special favorite of Freud's: "Until all the buttons are ripped from the pants of my patience."

18. Therefore one will hardly be able to reduce Freud's conceptual world to the common denominator of "simplification," that is, to the effort to replace the "complicated with the ever more simple" (thus Caruso).

19. From that viewpoint David Riesman's assertion that Freud's spirit aimed at the structuring of systems must also be designated a crude, if not erroneous, interpretation.

20. Arnold Gehlen praised Freud very highly for this reduction in the difference in levels between psychology in Wundt's time and artists like Proust, Musil, Flaubert, and Dostoevski, and called him a "Galileo of inner-world data."

21. "I went away with a full heart."

22. "We will not fall out of the world." This quotation from Grabbe's "Hannibal" was one of Freud's favorites.

23. We would like to emphasize this aspect in contrast to Fromm's incomprehensible and malicious assertion (*Sigmund Freud's Mission*) that for Freud there was no certainty in love but only in knowledge.

24. The suppression should not be confused with repression.

25. Hermann Adler goes so far as to explain Freud's teaching on unconscious processes on the basis of his being a Jew.

26. "A rationalist or perhaps analytical disposition within me struggles against my being deeply moved and not knowing why I am and what has moved me. . . . Such a work of art needs interpretation, and only after its completion can I learn why I am subject to so powerful an impression."

27. The only connection in which it seemed to play a role is the discovery of the Oedipus complex in himself. The whole business moved him so deeply and yet was also so repugnant to him that in the letter in which he reported it to his friend he fell into a mixture of German and Latin such as he had never used elsewhere (suggested here with English and Latin): ". . . that later my libido was awakened against *matrem* . . . because of . . . and on the occasion of my seeing her *nudam*." The feeling of guilt must have been so strong that after the death of his mother about seventy years after this incident, he reacted primarily with a "feeling of liberation, of acquittal."

NOTES

3. THE THEORY: POINTS OF DEPARTURE AND DISAGREEMENTS

1. Especially, no doubt, the relationship with his half brother.

2. Through the genetic method we reach a "clear and beautiful insight into the spiritual nature of humanity . . . if we follow the developmental process step by step" (Carus).

3. "When I noticed that you thought so much of me, I even used to think something of myself."

4. "Now, what is the physiological correlate of the simple or the recurring concept? Obviously not something at rest but something in the nature of a process. This process tolerates localization [according to the whole context, at this point a negative has apparently been omitted through typographical error; it should read "does not tolerate localization"]; it starts at a particular place in the cerebral cortex and spreads from there over the whole cerebral cortex or along particular paths."

5. "Thus we reach the point of assuming two classes of speech disturbances: (1) an aphasia of the first order, verbal aphasia, in which only the associations between the individual elements of the word concept are disturbed, and (2) an aphasia of the second order, asymbolic aphasia, in which the association of word and object concept is disturbed . . . because to me the relationship between word and object concept seems to earn the name of a 'symbolic' relationship more than that between object and object concept."

6. Karl Jaspers never took cognizance of this component of understanding in Freud; otherwise he could hardly have reproached him for having understood "only in the theorizing form of natural science instead of purely and freely" and of having thus fallen into a "confusing muddle of psychologizing theories."

7. This fact is overlooked by such critics as Igor Caruso, who asserts that Freud developed only a single theory, according to which the whole world is subject to the chemical laws of matter.

8. Jaspers, on the other hand, persistently held to the principle that human reality as a whole eludes our knowledge and cannot be put into language at all; therefore, psychoanalysis, which supposedly comprehends only a single aspect, must fail.

9. How little these concepts, which were dually conceived from the beginning, were understood, is shown by Peter Hoffstätter's assertion that in Freud's thinking it was not until after World War I that a "change from a one-drive theory to a dualistic system" was achieved.

10. According to the stipulations of Jung's will, the correspondence between him and Freud was not to be published until twenty years after his death, that is, until 1981.

11. It was thus precisely a question of the personal for Freud in his emphasis on the instinctive-emotional, and one misunderstands him completely if one throws him together with L. Klages in the pot of the

"irrationalists" and asserts that he turned humanity over to the "purely animal."

12. A supposedly trustworthy patient describes Jung's method of treatment in this way.

13. "Dreamwork does not calculate; it treats numbers like word concepts."

14. "Sometimes one could doubt whether the dragon of primeval times has really died out."

4. THE THERAPY: HEALING THROUGH LANGUAGE

1. See p. 16 above.

2. Thus Gehlen believes "that psychotherapy works well as individual psychology, poorly as social psychology," and "categories that are picked up from the psychic life of the individual are characteristically distorted and finally burst when overloaded with collective psychic content."

3. Heidegger, *Being and Time.* We discover here again Wilhelm Fliess's objection to Freud (see p. 59 above).

4. At this point one thinks especially of the rather widespread effect that the transference of Freudian thought processes has exercised in the area of social criticism through Herbert Marcuse and David Riesman.

5. For Freud this means nothing other than the replacement of the religious terminology of the past with the scientific terminology of the present.

6. "It is a great misfortune for me that nature did not give me that indefinite something that attracts people."

7. Freud borrowed this concept from Jung.

8. Thus Loch. Cf. Freud: "The assumptions of the doctor that miss the mark will be noticed in the course of the analysis and must be withdrawn and replaced by more correct ones."

9. See p. 90 above.

10. It is amazing that in spite of such clear statements, which can be demonstrated in Freud since 1900, the assertion repeatedly appears that Freud recognized the unconscious only as what was individually repressed.

11. Here we only point to the parallels with linguistic structures outside of "Standard Average European," as presented by Benjamin Lee Whorf in *Language, Thought, and Reality.*

5. THE APPLICATION: FREUD'S VIEWS ON RELIGION

1. As Rieff correctly emphasizes ("Meaning and History of Religion," 114), Freud's metapsychological speculations cannot, therefore, be regarded as decoration for his insights; they are rather an essential part and a necessary basis of those insights.

2. Among the few who today still stubbornly try to dispute the curative effect of psychoanalysis is Hans Jürgen Eysenck. He especially employs

the argument that there is still no statistical information on the effects of psychoanalysis. This, however, must be considered already refuted since the publication of the results of clinical treatment in the Berlin Psychoanalytic Institute, 1920–30, according to which in ninety-one percent of the cases in which the analysis could be terminated, an improvement or cure could be determined (published in Stafford-Clark, *What Freud Really Said*).

3. "Because of his rationalism, the philosophical efforts to which Freud's clinical discoveries led had to result in the worst idealistic aberrations" (Marc Oraison).

4. The most spirited and ingenious attack against such a position was without doubt led by William McDougall (*Psycho-analysis and Social Psychology*). He was followed by Arnold Gehlen, who considers Freud's theory appropriate for dreams and neuroses and in this dimension brilliant, but no longer convincing in its application to religion.

5. It is reported in detail in Riesman, "Freud and Psychoanalysis."

6. W. Kurth also believes he is able to discover congruence between the Freudian and the spiritual conceptions of humanity, and Fromm (*Forgotten Language*) points to the anthropological parallels between Augustine and Freud, which, to be sure, he thinks he must reject as one-sided.

7. V. von Weizsäcker reported a personal conversation with Freud in which he characterized his own position as related to mysticism because he believed that there are things that we cannot know, to which Freud is supposed to have replied: "Ah, so. In this case perhaps I go even further than you."

8. Thus Ludwig Marcuse, who points to the parallel between Freud and Meister Eckhart.

9. Arthur Guirdham's argument that Freud would not have fought so bitterly against God if he had not, in one part of his being, believed in God's existence, of course, seems too superficial. Even Hjalmar Sundén adopts the Freudian method by applying it to Freud himself: Sundén infers the repression of God from an error made by Freud, who in a quotation from Shakespeare mistakenly replaced the word "God" with "nature."

10. As far as I know, the key word "mysticism" appears only a single time in Freud, in a passing notice from his last days, in which he calls it the "dark perception by the self of the realm outside the ego."

11. See p. 27 above.

12. That the beginnings of legend formation can be seen even here is shown by the fact that Gregory Zilboorg speaks of five churches and accords a great significance to this number. His analysis is adopted by Sundén, but Freud himself makes no mention of it.

13. The enlightened Freud only once felt it necessary to make use of a superstitious formula. In 1899 he wrote to Fliess, "Only with the ——— feminine do I still not know at all how to begin." Not until 1931 was he able to make the decision to venture a summary presentation of feminine sexuality.

14. Of course, whether one can, with Velikovsky ("Dreams Freud Dreamt"), draw the conclusion that Freud suffered all his life from being a Jew and longed to be a Catholic seems extremely doubtful to me!

15. Freud himself believed the matter could be explained by the fact that every person has an immediate experiential relationship with his mother, whereas the fatherhood of the father is, from the very beginning, a question of "faith"!

16. This was the same year in which he encountered for the first time the Moses problem, from which he would not be able to free himself for the rest of his life.

17. It certainly does not apply to Far Eastern religions!

18. "It is not correct that since the earliest times the human soul has experienced no development and . . . is still the same as at the beginning of history."

19. "It is our best hope for the future that with time reason will come to power in the human soul."

20. A few years ago I myself still disregarded this perception and must herewith expressly correct myself.

21. Freud supports this theory with an observation from Goethe and research by E. Sellin.

6. THE CHALLENGE: PSYCHOANALYSIS AS CRITICISM OF RELIGION

1. Freud was probably thinking especially of Ludwig Feuerbach, Marx, and Nietzsche.

2. Freud maintained that the only arguments given on the part of religion in response to the critical inquiry into an authentication of the tenets of faith were the reference to the faith of the fathers, proofs handed down from antiquity, and finally the prohibition against throwing open such a question in the first place. He obviously did not realize at all what a caricature of genuine faith he was drawing. Yet one should consider that Freud did not maliciously invent his picture of religion but saw it largely realized in the world around him.

3. As to Viktor E. Frankl's remark—which borders on maliciousness—that Freud always "remained imprisoned to the, on the one hand, prudish, on the other, lustful spirit of the time," the first half, in any case, is true.

4. Freud's abruptness at this point can be blamed on this absolute moral integrity and not, as Fromm (*Sigmund Freud's Mission*) represents it, on his tyrannical impatience.

5. Rieff (*Freud*) has pointed most impressively to the fact that in Freud moral assumptions are to a large extent presupposed.

6. This is expressed especially neatly in an excerpt from a letter: "Germany will probably not become involved in our concern until some high muck-a-muck solemnly recognizes it. Perhaps the quickest way would

be for Kaiser Wilhelm, who of course understands everything, to take an interest in it!'

7. Erich Fromm (*Man for Himself*) sees this relativization of the phenomenon of conscience as a basic issue of our day in general.

8. Therefore one can scarcely make the reproach (as Igor Caruso does) that Freud's soul lacks what is essential, namely, a personal conscience, and that consequently he shares the faith of his time in the soullessness of people.

9. According to Arnold Gehlen this interpretation of neurosis as a kind of disease of the "social organism" is excellent and the starting point for further necessary reflections.

10. See p. 115 above.

11. Thus Freud held that religion was unchangeable but science was capable of unending perfection. Here reigned, apparently, one of Freud's gravest misunderstandings, for there are more than a few historians of religion who would be ready to turn this relationship completely around.

REFERENCES

Bultmann, Rudolf. *Faith and Understanding.* Vol. 1. New York: Harper & Row, 1969. Only the 1st of 5 vols. has appeared in English.
_____. *Jesus Christ and Mythology.* New York: Charles Scribner's Sons, 1958.
Freud, Sigmund. *The Standard Edition of the Complete Psychological Works of Sigmund Freud.* London: Hogarth Press, 1953–.
Freud, Sigmund, and Oskar Pfister. *Psychoanalysis and Faith: The Letters of Sigmund Freud and Oskar Pfister.* New York: Basic Books, 1964.
Fromm, Erich. *The Forgotten Language: An Introduction to the Understanding of Dreams, Fairy Tales, and Myths.* New York: Rinehart & Co., 1951.
_____. *Man for Himself.* New York: Rinehart & Co., 1947.
_____. *Sigmund Freud's Mission.* New York: Harper & Bros., 1959.
Heidegger, Martin. *Being and Time.* New York: Harper & Row, 1962.
Heisenberg, Werner. *Physics and Philosophy.* New York: Harper & Row, 1962.
Jones, Ernest. *The Life and Work of Sigmund Freud.* 3 vols. New York: Basic Books, 1953–57.
Kemp, Charles F. *Physicians of the Soul.* New York: Macmillan Co., 1947.
Lee, R. S. *Freud and Christianity.* New York: A. A. Wyn, 1949.
McDougall, William. *Psycho-analysis and Social Psychology.* London: Methuen & Co., 1936.
Merlan, Philip. "Brentano and Freud." *Journal of the History of Ideas* 6 (1945): 375–77.
Mill, John Stuart. "Grote's Plato." In *Collected Works of John Stuart Mill* 2:375–440. Toronto: Univ. of Toronto Press, 1978.
Murray, J. A. C. *An Introduction to Christian Psychotherapy.* Edinburgh: T. & T. Clark, 1947.
Outler, Albert D. *Psychotherapy and the Christian Message.* New York: Harper & Bros., 1954.

REFERENCES

Pfister, Oskar. *The Psychoanalytic Method.* New York: Moffat, Yard & Co., 1917.

Rieff, Philip. *Freud: The Mind of the Moralist.* New York: Viking Press, 1959.

———. "The Meaning of History and Religion in Freud's Thought." *Journal of Religion* 31 (1951): 114–31.

———. *The Triumph of the Therapeutic.* New York: Harper & Row, 1966.

Riesman, David. "Freud and Psychoanalysis." In *Individualism Reconsidered,* 305–408. Glencoe, Ill.: Free Press, 1954.

Salter, Andrew. *The Case against Psychoanalysis.* New York: Henry Holt & Co., 1952.

Stafford-Clark, David. *What Freud Really Said.* New York: Schocken Books, 1967.

Tillich, Paul. *The Courage to Be.* New Haven: Yale Univ. Press, 1952.

———. *Love, Power, and Justice.* New York: Oxford Univ. Press, 1954.

———. *Systematic Theology.* 3 vols. Chicago: Univ. of Chicago Press, 1951–63.

Velikovsky, I. "The Dreams Freud Dreamt." *Psychoanalytic Review* 28 (1941): 487–511.

Whorf, Benjamin Lee. *Language, Thought, and Reality.* Cambridge: MIT Press, 1956.

INDEX

INDEX

Delusion, 135–36, 140, 145
Demons, 39, 70, 86, 122, 127
Depression, 3, 85, 103
Destiny, 41, 46–47, 52, 54, 55, 106,
  118, 130
Doctor, 1, 10, 17, 22, 28, 52, 85, 87,
  89–91, 94, 97, 134
Dreams, 15, 18, 30, 33, 35, 39, 60,
  71–75, 100–101, 116, 136, 138–39

Ego, 9, 18, 36, 46, 54, 55, 62–67, 74–75,
  86, 94, 102, 113, 128–29, 131–32,
  135, 137, 139, 145
Empiricism, 8, 12, 68, 73, 140
Epistemology, 4, 20, 38
Eros, 51–52, 65, 91, 119, 128–29, 132,
  134, 145
  and Ananke, 35, 66, 135
Ethics, 6, 8, 11, 13–14, 20, 30, 44, 48,
  92, 113, 116, 122, 123, 125–27,
  130–32, 135
  sexual, 20, 35
Existentialism, 2, 20, 21, 24, 42, 80–82,
  103–6, 123, 137

Faith, 2, 4, 5, 9, 12, 15, 17–18, 23, 24,
  35, 36, 38, 41, 43–44, 83–84, 99,
  104–5, 109, 111–12, 116–19, 123,
  125, 130–31, 135, 143, 145
  Christian, 7, 18–19, 21, 24, 77, 114,
  123, 125, 142
Family, 31, 32, 78
Fantasy, 5, 11, 18–19, 60–61, 71, 90,
  101–2, 106
Fate, 20, 55, 79, 119, 131, 143
Father, 19, 27, 43–44, 54, 61, 68, 91,
  109–10, 111, 113–15, 128–30,
  141–42
Fear, 11, 52, 61
Fliess, Wilhelm, 30, 56–59, 61,
  62–63, 109
Fratricide, 130
Free association, 34, 71
Freedom, 13, 18–19, 23, 49, 67, 75, 84,
  86, 93–94, 103, 105, 126, 127,
  131–32, 145
Fuchs, Ernst, xi, xiii, 103–6

God, 7, 15–16, 17, 24, 27, 36, 41, 77,
  80–82, 104–6, 108, 111, 118, 122,
  127, 130, 134, 141, 143–45
Gomperz, Theodor, 29–30, 36
Guilt, 4, 12–13, 23, 47, 48, 113–14, 116,
  123, 129, 141–42

Hate, 49, 65, 69, 129, 132
Healing, 76, 85, 90–91, 99, 103, 107,
  119, 126, 134–35
Heidegger, Martin, xiv, 12, 20, 79–80,
  82–84, 104–5, 127
Helmholtz, Hermann, 31, 50, 56
Hermeneutics, xiii, 6, 22, 23, 46, 72–73,
  77–78, 83–84, 92, 95–96, 99, 103–5
  circle, 46, 74, 83–84, 89, 92, 96
  principle, 81, 84, 103, 138
  theological, 80–81, 99
History, xiii, 4, 5, 7, 12, 18, 20, 23–25,
  34, 35, 36, 40, 47, 48, 52, 53, 55,
  56, 69, 72, 75, 76, 79, 81, 83–84,
  94–95, 99, 101, 102, 104–5, 109,
  112, 115, 120–23, 127, 130,
  132–33, 140, 141, 142–43, 145
  ahistorical, 67, 69, 102, 112, 120,
  142, 143, 145
  case, 38, 134
  of human existence, 20, 25, 53, 81,
  118, 128–29, 135, 139
  personal, 3, 16, 87, 102, 113, 135
  primal, and prehistory, 34, 58,
  112–13, 115, 128, 140, 144
Holy Spirit, 12, 21, 23, 27
Hypnosis, 32, 50, 85, 87
Hysteria, 32, 39, 50–51, 58, 66, 71–72,
  86–87, 89, 95, 99, 100, 125, 137–38

Id, 9, 36, 62, 75, 139, 143
Ideology, 8, 9, 11, 15–17, 20, 24, 36–37,
  64, 69, 76, 131
  ideological suspicion, 15, 20, 36, 77
Illness, 11, 15, 22, 28, 32, 51, 79, 91,
  99–100, 102, 127, 137
  psychotic, 52, 63, 86, 101, 135–36
Illusion, 8, 9, 23, 37, 38, 47, 57, 81, 83,
  90, 98, 107, 116–17, 124–25, 133,
  140, 144
Impulse, 55, 98, 118, 141, 143
Infantilism, 23, 54, 63, 91, 101, 111,
  117–18, 120, 123, 137, 142, 144
Instincts, 46, 47, 52, 53, 55–56, 62–68,
  73, 91, 111, 118, 126–29, 131, 137,
  143
  destruction, 119, 129, 131
  ego, 63–65, 67
  sexual, 64–66
Interpretation, 73–74, 88, 94–95, 97,
  138–40

Jesus Christ, 7–8, 12, 97, 104–5,
  114, 143

159

INDEX